A BIRTHRIGHT

RECEIVED

Philip Scott

Dedication

To my dear wife Kitty. I can only marvel at how you have been used to contribute to my spiritual maturity as a man in Christ. Through our many discussions and prayers together we have witnessed revelations upon our lives and others. With this, my life has witnessed the grace and mercy of God. The words he has provided you to speak to me have been blessings, though hard to receive many times during this growth, they were intended to spiritually mature me as a child of God. You are greatly loved and appreciated beyond words. Thank you, Kitty.

I dedicate this book to my brothers and sisters in Christ. I offer it to all whom may ever read it desiring complete submission to the Lord. I hope that the children I have brought into this world will consume it and pass it down to those they bring into the world and those they come across. Amaiya, Gianna, Lily and my son Andrew. This book was written for you. This is my inheritance I pass down to you. Look after each other and love one another with the word of God. To my mother Judith, thank you for your wisdom and correction from my youth to my adulthood. Thank you for such priceless prayers on my behalf. My brother in the faith, Edwin. You are valued and sincere in your walk. Your family is blessed because of you and I'm thankful for you.

I have not always loved you all the right way. It's because I have not always known the father. The creator of all things in heaven and earth. This means I never knew his son, which means I never knew true love. But God. My God! His infinite compassion showed me mercy and his grace gave me the chance to witness the truth not just in words alone, but in action. You see, I believed the lie like many have. The lie that life was about me. What I want, what I prefer, and if anyone conflicts with that, they are my enemy. This was easy to believe because I never understood my birthright. It is the same right every single person has on planet earth. That is the right to the **truth.** Not just any truth, or any truth catered to what you like or desire in life for yourself, but the truth in Christ. The truth God wanted us all to have from birth. This is our birthright. I hope to give that truth to everyone as I now understand it by God's grace. There is no purpose in life outside of it. What a gift it is to receive your birthright.

Love always, Philip

A Birthright Received

Contents

Preface

This book will not be the longest book ever written. It may not contain any new information for the person well versed in scripture. It was not written to accomplish some lofty goal to sound profound as I am not the best writer. Nor do I have the best education. I am a man with a past of evil and wickedness. Deep and profound lostness consumed my youth and adulthood. I existed with no moral compass or integrity, yet proudly claimed Christ. Then once my marriage was fractured and corrupted by my lustful and self-centered desires, I heard the voice of God. It wasn't an encouraging voice though it proved to be more than I could have imagined. Nor was it one that prophesied a great future for me, but one of correction and truth about who I was currently and who I had always been. I searched the scriptures to see if what I was hearing was from God and found this in **Revelation 3:19. To those I love, I rebuke and discipline, therefore be earnest and repent.** This was my confirmation! What I heard was the voice of God. His voice clearly told me that I **never** knew him. No matter how many water baptisms I got could clean me and no amount of crying would change this truth. He said that no matter how much I talked about him or wrote things concerning him could change that if I didn't align my life with his word. This rebuke led to an honest repentance and daily discipline to align my mind and life with truth. I sought him with all my heart and his promise proved true. Then my actions and words found the will of God and he guided them. So, I began to write what I heard as I read scripture. This is why this book exists. It was written to expose the very deceptive ways I found myself lost in while claiming to be a follower of Christ. It was written to bring light to dark times that are going to get darker. It was written to show no matter how dark it gets; the light will always expose it. The light will always reign above it. For each person must choose the light. The light is hard to receive because many of us have been convinced that truth is merely a subjective reality, based on our own experiences. The light is hard to receive for we have all been born into sin. That sin is a self-centered, selfish nature that desires everything to be about us. Our own preferences, our own desires, our own understandings. This is the deception that comes from the pit of hell. A lie orchestrated by an enemy that wishes to keep all from the **real truth**.

You see, the enemy is aware that there is **one truth**. He just hates it. Now with that, every effort is made by the enemy to construct a reality of falsehoods that play upon the mind. **This enemy I speak of is within us, for it is us**. For it is us that rejected God from the beginning. Introducing a spirit of rebellion into the world. The lie is that Satan is somehow separate from man. Yet the truth is, man is the serpent. Isn't it interesting that the bible never mentions the serpent being kicked out of the garden of Eden? He didn't have to kick the serpent out specifically because the two that had the serpent within them were being kicked out. So much is made of the devil yet the biblical information we are given in how to defend ourselves against him is to simply resist him. You would think there was some lofty fight required against this powerful being. No, he will flee upon you resisting which tells me he is a way of thinking that is against God.

That same serpent is what compels many today. The voice of rebellion against what God has said. It is our own logic and craftiness thereof that is like a serpent. It strikes without warning and deceives with crafty mental rationalizations and justifications. The very adoption and acceptance of such a mind is Satan himself. With that said, understand this. What God put in place can never be removed. It brings peace and freedom to all that accept his truth as their own. To those that accept and choose to receive falsehoods as truth, they effectively clothe themselves in selfishness and pride as their truth. Once this is done, selfishness and pride will desire to be glorified. For it will serve as their God. For God's way clearly states what we are not to agree in thought with. What we are not to act upon. The very rebellion against his way displays whom we follow. To be clear, our rebellion follows lies and destruction. When this is done, we have given ourselves over to what pleases them. Having now decided to directly dismiss the consequences, life deceives itself to believe there will be none. The deception that comes along with this is that the pleasures of sin are more valuable, and freeing than the truth in Christ Jesus. The truth is there is no freedom and no value in a walk of life apart from Christ. There is only freedom in Christ Jesus. There is only peace in Christ Jesus. His freedom and peace are not as the world offers them. So, the world cannot comprehend its value.

The world's way of thinking will harden our thoughts and kill the hunger to listen to Christ. This book desires to detail how it does that and how you can truly desire a heart after God.

This book will speak to the fact that if we do not nurture the truth through the teachings of Christ Jesus we won't be baptized by fire, thereby no resurrection will be possible.

Essentially within ourselves, we cannot produce any good thoughts or actions. **All our ways are evil and wicked.** We need the Holy Spirit. The Spirit we have is of rebellion. This is why being born again is required. The seeds we use daily produce spoiled; rotten fruit clothed in stains of blood from others we come across. The only way to clean such is by pure and undefiled blood. This was sent by the Creator, the Most High God through Jesus Christ. He provided the food and the water. Reminding us of the seed planted from God the Father from the beginning. Your mind is the soil. This may sound confusing, but Christ gave his body as the food and his words are the water. You must believe in the sacrifice of his body as the one single thing that can make you right with God and invest in his words to truly nurture your seed. Only then can you produce the right fruit. When he says you must consume his flesh, he is saying this belief in him must be **inside of you**. This is how we become one with the only true living God. Our Father. He came for all that will submit to his will. To stand against whom they once were. Those that will accept that they are sick and lost instead of in good health and home. For without our Lord, I wouldn't know the only way to him, no one would. I would have just been content in the ways of my past. Only wanting to correct those ways for my own comfort of living. With all things, he uses all things for good for those that truly love and trust in him. Let us truly believe, walk in his peace and his freedom now, and receive his promises with his Holy Spirit. Have no fear for if God is for us, whom be against us?! No matter the power, nor the weapon formed in this world. Neither can conquer us because our Father, through his son Jesus, provides freedom, peace, and life eternally. It is our birthright that we receive this truth and believe in it. I hope and pray this be a birthright received!

KNOW THE TRUTH AND BE SET FREE

A

Birthright

Received

‏רִאשׁוֹן‏ (rishon)

<u>Life knowledge</u>

As I begin, it is important to remember that the contents of the Holy Bible explain your birthright. In the scriptures, the birthright usually refers to **the right of the son born first in a family to inherit his father's possessions and authority.** For your birthright is to receive the truth of God in Christ. Jesus Christ is the first-born son of God. Be not confused by this statement, we hear it a lot, but many don't truly understand what it means. So, to be clear. Jesus lived his entire life completely submitted to the Father who is Spirit. The Father, who is a Spirit, has a character that is love and a Spirit that encompasses the traits of love. God anointed Jesus with his Spirit to carry out the very power he has here on earth, because of his complete submission to him and his ways. Therefore, he is called the son of God. His very words and teachings are very direct. They state that we must be born again. For he was born spiritually from God. He exposed the lie and the corruption of man within their own hearts. Seeing this they could do nothing against him in truth so the evil one from within them needed to silence him. Though they were able to take his physical life upon a cross, in three days that very beaten and disregarded body would awaken and rise from death. This signified without any dispute in the heavens and earth to those who love God that his

Birthright was received as the first-born son of God. Here is the good news!! If we believe in his son, Jesus Christ. God adopts us as children into that same Birthright! To receive this Birthright of eternal life one must truly believe in their heart all of this, meaning a true repentance must occur. Then a life will be lived that reflects the very same traits Jesus has. The very life of that person will be saved from the fate that will come upon the wicked spirit that deceived the world. This is life knowledge.

Christ knowledge is life

There are many books written in this world. Many that hold vast amounts of information. Information about every single aspect of life and the things within it. Then we have the Bible. This collection of writings from men over a course of thousands of years detailing the events and experiences they had and witnessed during their time on earth. It details historical events that took place, and it also details the core foundation of mankind. The deceptions that have existed from the beginning. It encompasses wisdom and valuable information on how to live with the right heart. It speaks to the difficulties and the sins of men prior. More importantly it details how God has put in place a perfect plan to save mankind from its coming fate. The very fate that is coming due to the rebellion and rejection of him. No-one can dismiss this collection of writings; they can only reject them. It is the first and the last book to depict our Lord. It also provides an accurate depiction of all mankind.

Now as for these other books in the world that hold their knowledge, they attempt to copy the format so to speak of the Holy Bible. Instead of providing information of life in Christ, they detail a deceiving form of life. That deceiving form of life comes in various ways. The centralized focus used by many comes from topics such as specific ways to live on earth, ways to have a better life on earth, how to gain wealth, how to have better relationships, etc. This means there are two forms of knowledge out in the world. One about God and one about how to live a life here on earth that tries to manipulate God for our own desires. Both believers and non-believers indulge in such knowledge. Some of the things that come from death knowledge can be helpful if **not** idolized. This is only possible if you have life knowledge prior to it. For the knowledge of life can give a pulse to death knowledge. Sadly, the risk taken by reading such books is that the line of idolization can become very thin and crossed without knowing it. It is important to understand that it is just not life knowledge, meaning it should not be the focus of your understanding. This is hard to receive because many of these sorts of books specifically speak to how to live and that confuses many as being life knowledge. To examine this statement, consider this instance. Think about a cookbook. That book will detail recipes on how to make several different meals. There is no error in a cookbook to harm your soul. Now let's consider if that cookbook falls into the hands of a glutton. That person already idolizes food and seeks it for comfort even. That cookbook now becomes a hindrance to such a person. This shows that wisdom in Christ (life knowledge) must be obtained prior to this knowledge, yes even knowledge on how to prepare a meal. If anything, the extreme nature of this reality is only made true because of the fallen nature of man. For recipes alone can be a stumbling block to a glutton, because man idolizes everything it desires. It isn't the cookbook that is in error but rather the reader. It is the reader that does not have the Bible as the focus of their life, so any information read can be corrupted into a form of knowledge that seeks life yet will produce death. This is the deception from within. Mankind seeks life where there is no life and seeks it in the things of this world. This is what I mean by death knowledge. Any knowledge attained in place of life knowledge which is in Christ.

Do not underestimate the worldly power Satan has over many. For by the hand of a man without life knowledge in Christ, words of foolishness are written. Those words can be read for years to come and populate a generation of fools for generations. Foolishly seeking what they can perceive as good or profitable yet following darkness. Now if the words of the unwise have power. How much greater is the power through the words written ordained by the light? Those words will shine upon those who write in the dark and reveal theirs as false. It will also reveal itself as truth in the process. Further-more inspiring those of a generation that seeks the light to see exactly where their true beginning was and therefore giving them a foundation to stand on. So, to better understand these two forms of knowledge they must be revealed. Christ was sent to reveal the knowledge of God and that wisdom is of life. That wicked spirit that is against God known as Satan, presents his wisdom of death to the world. If you do not know Christ truly, the wisdom of Satan can mask itself as a form of good and profitable knowledge that is not wrong to gain. Please see the book of Genesis where Eve makes it clear that the act of disobedience can appear desirable through knowledge of what is good and evil.

Find out what you truly seek

To truly seek what is incorruptible, there must be a want for no corruption. Within a man is where his light resides. This is where all corruption seeks to dwell. Darkness cannot do anything against the light. In John 1:4-5 it says, **"The Word gave life to everything that was created, and his life brought light to everyone. The light shines in the darkness, and the darkness can never extinguish it".** We must willfully agree with darkness so that light is dimmed within us. Yet even still the light exists. The light is not made true because of us. It is true regardless. The worst part about death is knowing only it and never knowing true life in Christ. Usually, most know this death while breathing. Confusing it as life because the grave has yet to be inhabited. Yet the anger of knowing that the truth is conflicting with darkness for most is why true life is rejected. This is because death has disguised itself as life for this generation. Now consider that many in this world desire connections/relationships while operating under this disguise. Many times, without any knowledge, they are in disguise.

It would be better to find yourself first in Christ than find another and not know who you are. The chances of turning into who you meet when you don't know who you are in Christ first is very high. Therefore, seeking first the Kingdom of God is key. So be careful. Christ provides you with your identity in God before any interaction can attempt to mold you. The mind and body must become one. Yes, within oneself. For one can seek life and the other could be content with the ways of death. What sorrow precedes watching a loved one die or live in death contently. Take heed to this advice. Learn about love. Learn it from the one that spoke directly to it and gave it as a commandment. This will expose who you are without Christ and how God truly views you if you are living outside of him. This will truly bring attention to the desires within your heart, revealing them as having no desire for God. You will find your heart is where the lust resides and where your destruction is. No-one living knows the depths of one's thoughts outside of their own. How hesitant we are to reveal every thought we have had as we know the darkness in them. So, learn the ways of God and examine if your ways are pure. For everything within you is what determines if you are in life with Christ or in death and deceived.

We are what we agree with

"Be not deceived; God is not mocked: for whatsoever a man soweth, that shall he also reap."

Everything you **see plants images** into the **soul.** So, let the images be full of **light**. For if they are dark then the soul will not be able to see its way back to the Holy Light. Forms of darkness give birth to things such as **stress, fatigue, frustration, anger, worldly desire, jealousy,** and things of that nature. This becomes your normal. Live **not** for the body, but rather for the spirit. That is what can live forever with your Father in Heaven. The soul that lives in you is from The Father in Heaven. He grants life and a life source we know as oxygen. He is the only one that grants life sources. Water, food, along with vegetation are all from the one who is life. So, we live on this planet that sustains life sources and we use them to live. Yet our nature of being or way of living is from this world. When a statement like this is made, it's not a reference to the planet. Rather it is to a way of thinking and living created by those who have rejected God and desire those ways for others. A world that has turned away from God and delights in its darkness and its deception. The Creator of the universe is of unman made lights. All the wonderful lights you see unmatched by man came from The God that is pure. So, you see darkness is simply the absence of The Father who is light. This is key for he brought us forth from his light. What we see now is a generation that is choosing to reject that light and seek their own, but without him there is no other light, just darkness. Once this was realized in the beginning of rebellion, fear came over us. So now fear is amongst rebellion, and neither are from God. Mankind has done this constantly to God from that point on. We reject him then we hide. Is there any mystery why in revelations **cowards** are the **first** to be cast into the lake of fire?! I don't think we even consider this enough. See Revelations 21:8. This exposes our true fallen nature. We are ashamed of what our new form of being is without the light of God. Now you see arrogance and pride boasting of its ways apart from God. Some even claim to be in alignment with him while living in those ways. It is very heartbreaking to witness this. I believe God wants to reveal this within us **first** before seeing it in others. The purpose of our existence is not to be confused. When you remove the light from our understanding, confusion enters, and only darkness remains. Living pure and loving others is key; for this is what will return to The Father when the soul he gave us leaves this flesh. The condition of that soul he gave can only return to him if it is of him. If that soul did not have his Holy Spirit guiding it, it is not of him. It must go where he is not. Your choice, given by God as free will, is proof through your actions and your actions are proven by what you truly seek. Be not deceived, we all will reap our ways, and thoughts we have displayed internally and externally. The Heavenly Father is just, and it is only right to give to a person what they have desired. I plead for all to desire life knowledge so that you might live. Death knowledge cannot inform you of anything but itself. Do not think that this life is about anything other than people choosing life or death. I say this because we all shall take our turn to meet the grave. If you only desired knowledge of death and lived your life through that, you do not have the knowledge to be raised from it. It is the Christ Jesus that stated until the mind and body become one you cannot see heaven. Therefore, all that lived with the mind of death simply remain in that knowledge for eternity. As for those who have lived with the knowledge of life, Jesus has informed us we will be raised for eternity in such with him. Choose today which knowledge you desire eternity with.

שֵׁ נִ י (sheni)

The conflict

Yeshua The Christ was prophesied to come and to give us all the light, the truth. The world you reside in knows no truth if it is not in him. It only knows its strategic lies that have artificially created its own way of existence. Seek not what it says is the way. For many say there are many ways to Heaven. Yet not one person has been there, so how can they speak about how to get there? What they say about finding

God always looks to appeal to a persons' preference. Those same people even include those who do not believe in God at all as those who can enter heaven. It is clear those who speak in such a way are more concerned about keeping each person comfortable in how they live. The fear of conflict. Well, this belief in Christ Jesus who was sent from God is not for cowards. It is for those who are not ashamed and are willing to accept the worldly consequences that may come because of the truth. Those who speak deceptively to others about this would never lay their life down for what they claim. Give not a second of your time to those without backbones for the truth. Give every second God grants you to the only one that has been to Heaven, and that has seen God. This is the only one who can inform us how to do both. His name is The Christ, which is derived from the Greek term Christos, which was translated from the

Hebrew term Ha-Mashiach the Messiah. The name Jesus is a Latin transliteration of the Hebrew name Yeshua which is a common name. The name not common is the **Christ. That's the name** that is key. For it means in Hebrew **One who is anointed**. The prophesied one that was to come. Yeshua the Ha-Mashiach, specifies whom the Lord is. Let no one corrupt you with translations as to consider one above the other. With that said, the Hebrew language is unlike any other and it is the language of the original chosen people by God. Nonetheless, God is the one who brought forth different languages at the tower of Babel. God is the one who displayed his Holy Spirit in different tongues on the day of Pentecost, and every man there heard worship of God in his own language. So whatever dialect of your choice just remember Jesus is the anointed one from God, he is the Messiah. The Heavenly Father anointed him with his

Holy Spirit to carry out his works here on earth. The mind must receive this to understand the truth. They both operate together just as your mind operates in your body to produce actions and words you choose. Christ spoke what the Father told him to speak and did what his Father desired him to do. He was submitted completely. So, when you pray, pray for the wisdom that rejects the world and its ways. Ask for the understanding of his word and not the things of this world. Pray for truth in Christ to be received so that his peace, his joy, and knowledge may be your desires. Be submitted completely just as he was and is. **Following him is living how he lived**. Once your heart is truly invested in this, you will seek to be baptized by water as to follow the path Jesus did so that your true birth can take place. Now simply being immersed in water will not be sufficient alone. That event is to show others your decision to turn from sin.

It is supposed to be a funeral to your living in sin and birth to start living righteously. Many have this event alone and do not truly get baptized by water, meaning the word of God. See to truly be borne by water is to live new according to it. This truly symbolizes the new life beginning. What manner of liquid water dismisses the necessity of learning the ways of God? I tell you the truth, many dismiss the word of God and claim the liquid water to be sufficient alone. I have been baptized 3 times, each time hoping to cleanse my conscience of living against God. Then the Lord spoke clearly to me. Until you desire me in your heart according to my word you are only putting on a show for yourself, and others with the water. Let my word be the water that baptizes you. Immerse yourself in it with your living Philip. This helped me understand what the water baptism is. Then I understood the baptism by fire Jesus came to bring. If anyone understands this must be done with a **sincere heart,** they will speak the truth and will confess that Yeshua the Christ is the son of God. This will grant you the gift of grace and mercy from God and he will send you The Holy Spirit. This will begin a pruning process of your life. More than speaking in tongues or the ability to articulate to others deep things of God. Your very life will begin to be altered. What was once, cannot be moving forward. Your mind must stay refreshed on his word to keep yourself present with your new life and new way of thinking. **This must be nurtured and not neglected**. You will find conflict in this information as many have, for it will challenge your desire for it. Your desire to live it I should say. Your flesh mind will not naturally want this information. Nonetheless, this will bring to the surface the need for the Holy Spirit. Many reject this baptism by fire that Jesus does because it challenges every fabric of your being to be conformed into his righteousness. Your flesh will attempt to cling to things in the world if you still have desires there.

The Holy Spirit reveals all truth

The Holy Spirit, despite what many may think they know of him, is a power that resides with those that believe truly and **live** as though they believe. Meaning, when life doesn't flow with comfort, they look like Christ during his discomfort. This is displayed in times of distress for anyone can present themselves as peaceful when everything in life is going according to their comfort level. You will notice those with the Holy Spirit have been given a clear mentality that focuses on the Lord and are comforted in those times. Clear thinking in this flesh to value the things of heaven above the things of this world. Their desires are different from those of this world. They speak differently and respond differently to things the world cannot understand. The Holy Spirit is what changes your mind on all things. It helps you remember what Christ said and guides you to discern things of this world that may attempt to deceive you. Without the Holy Spirit, a person is deceived daily by Satan. They have no way to operate with the mind of Christ for they struggle daily with the things of this world. The ideas of God are rejected without The Holy Spirit. The very words of God are rejected by all without the Holy Spirit. Many are deceived in thinking they have this Spirit that is Holy. This Spirit is here to reveal all truth to those who say they believe in Christ and is here to remind them of his words. Some examples of when I heard the Spirit speak to me is when I hear harsh truths. Direct instructions on what is right and what is wrong. My way of living and speaking are combed through with an examination to reveal who I am displaying at every given moment. I have noticed many want a Holy Spirit that comforts them in sin. As if God somehow aligns with that way of living. No-one ought to consider such blasphemy even remotely, but it is the unfortunate norm.

This Spirit is a comforting guide to live in righteousness. One that keeps his mind on Jesus amongst everyday life knows this Spirit. He is not here to be a sidekick to the lives the flesh desires. Rather an agent of our Lord. So, if you are in a situation where you are angry, you should hear; be at peace and do not speak through your anger. If you are in a situation where you have friends that are still doing things you have chosen not to do, then you should hear; be wise with your company. Bad company corrupts good morals. Again, the Holy Spirit is here to guide us in living righteous lives. Everyone's life is at different stages, some are in similar stages, but the Holy Spirit will speak to the heart that desires godliness in it. To the one that does not, he grieves the Holy Spirit as one claiming ignorance concerning what is right according to God. As it is written in Ephesians 4, do not grieve the Holy Spirit essentially with your conduct.

His Holy Spirit reveals you

The fruit or shall I say the ways of being that show you are a child of God are present with the one whose heart is pure. Unfortunately, many try to display these traits such as **peace**, **love**, **gentleness, joy, patience, long-suffering, self-control, kindness, and modesty** without a pure heart from God. These traits can be displayed **without** the right motives. With the Holy Spirit, the motive is your way of being that honors God. That way of being is not possible without The Holy Spirit as these things are from him. This shows the wickedness of the heart. It will try to mimic the ways of God to deceive others. For who would welcome a wolf to their dinner table? No-one but other wolves. So, the wolves know a mask is required, to get close to the sheep. Satan delights being in disguise for he knows his true self is not appealing to those in Christ. I have always found it deeply interesting that Jesus warned us of wolves in sheep clothing. When it comes to people these were the only ones, he warned us of. Open agents of the devil are not our concern, rather those that pose as brothers and sisters in Christ. Those are truly the enemy as they come to alter the word of God for others. They expose many to a false understanding of the truth and create a false image of God to the world. It is truly Satan and his demons most focused work. What is near and dear to me is the message I have been sent to proclaim in these last days. That message is to send a warning and an alarm to those claiming Christ, that the true end is near and the deception I found myself in must be exposed! We are to be aware of wolves in sheep's clothing but more than that we are to be aware that **we** are not the wolf in sheep clothing! This is the deception I found myself in. Claiming to be of Christ but my life, and my fruit was wicked and even greater in my opinion than lost non-believers. This is the message I am instructed to give. Examine your heart and your motives thoroughly now while you have a chance. Taking the Lords' name in vain is a great sin. I urge you in his name to examine your very life to ensure it aligns with his word. For the time is at hand that everyone will be exposed.

Fruits of the Spirit under attack

The Holy Spirit grants gifts and my goodness are they under attack. The gifts of the Holy Spirit range from **wisdom**, **understanding, counsel, fortitude, knowledge**, **piety**, and **the fear of the Lord**. So, these gifts given by the spirit are with you for eternity and the price you pay for them is dying daily to the flesh. As you grow in your walk with Christ you will desire such a death and see it as a necessary benefit. Now, the world has its gifts to offer also, but those things only exist temporarily. The world's gifts always come with a significant price in your life if idolized. That price is your life. The gifts of the world aren't even worthy of mentioning, for which is worth a life? Make no mistake, both gifts will cost you your life. So, consider why you would desire anything other than the gifts of the spirit. Christ informed us in Luke 14:28-29 that we ought to think about what is required of us if we decide to follow him. Whether it be the fruits of the Holy Spirit or the gifts of the Holy Spirit both will expose your heart as being not from him if you try to manipulate them for your gain here on earth. It appears many are using the gifts of the Holy Spirit to disregard the fruits. Let me be very clear about this. God will use your gifts to help others come to him, but if you do not have the fruits of the Spirit your very gifts will do nothing for you when judged by God. Many ignore this as their hearts are deceived. Living deceived, many seek things from this walk with Christ while claiming to seek Christ alone. They seek to glorify themselves above God. Inwardly having a hatred for him and his ways as it conflicts with theirs. He is not surprised by this as he has already prophesied it. This is simple the conflict of the flesh trying to manipulate the Spirit for its own desires. You might ask, why would someone do that? Or if they wanted the things of the world, why not just be in the world and go after those things. Why use the name of God through Jesus to get such things of the world? Well, these are very good questions and they prove to us that Satan is very real. Scripture tells us that in these last days he has transformed himself into an angel of light. This means his greatest deception is to appear as good. So while many encompass this wicked spirit, it comes upon many that claim Christ when they read the word of God and find no value in it outside of what appeals to the flesh. By that I mean this. God desires everyone but everyone does not desire God. So, when the Holy Spirit searches a person and finds the world and desires of the flesh, which usually has pride within it, God is far from them. Their attempt to draw near him was not to love him, but rather love of the world. Essentially the took the information as a tool rather than transformational knowledge. They use it as a tool to continue accomplishing their desires for the world. Not as knowledge to deny and reject it. I have unfortunately experienced this deception. Again, I am trying to expose it so you don't fall as I have. Now, being brought forth from such a darkness I can only believe I have been spared to expose this to all whom will listen. So how do I know if the motives for following God are worldly? As simple as this may seem, it is if your life does not conform to his righteousness. **If you are knowingly living in sin that the word of God speaks against and/or your behavior is not bearing fruit, that's the sign your motive is not love for God**. You have sought God with another agenda. God in his perfect grace and mercy will lay upon our hearts heavy with regret and feelings of condemnation in attempt to get our attention. Many think this is Satan doing this. Do we not understand that those God loves he rebukes and disciplines. Now the evil one will come during this process and make you will feel like you cannot turn to God but the heaviness upon your heart while living in sin is the love of God. If you do not grieve your ways, how do you even know your desire is to turn from them? Are we not aware that those in the world take no consideration for their ways as they do them against God? So, if you are living in sin that you are aware of and you have nothing upon your heart that has any feelings of regret or sorrow, you are illegitimate as it is written. For God has given you over to your flesh desires. Those he loves are always corrected and disciplined to transform their very lives into righteousness. Whether you are exposed here on earth or in judgment afterwards you will be exposed. I hope that no one is in this current position as I was, but I know of many that are. My hope is that you experience what I have, and that's being exposed for thinking you were of God, and finding you were not. I hope many come to this truth because it will save your life. If you happen to get this revelation about yourself, drop to your knees and thank him for his love! For by it he has loved you deeply to save you from a deception that will plague thousands! I hope you experience his mercy, and that is the ability to genuinely turn from the lie by his grace. To give you proper context of how deceived one can be. I held firm to the idea I knew God because of the way I could talk about him with others or write about him. Yet my life was consumed by lies, lust, deceit and ultimately came to a head through an affair I committed in my marriage. I truly did not see myself as one that did not know God, even while sleeping with married women, indulging in marijuana and alcohol, lying daily and displaying rages of anger towards loved ones including my children. All of this while maintaining unforgiveness and hatred in my heart towards my mother, the mothers of my children and my wife. Now how lost can one person be, to think they know God and produce such wickedness at the same time. This brings sorrow of depths without the ability to explain. I believe that God does this exposing in private for some and others publicly. If this is done to give anyone clarity while still here, then I pray you'd be so fortunate to witness that grace and mercy as I have.

When I realized I was using gifts of the Holy Spirit with the wrong motives and living in ways that were not of God, a very deep sorrow came over me. This is the deep sorrow I live with daily when my mind remembers it, for many were hurt and/or deceived by me. It is truly my thorn and it comes with a messenger of Satan. Reading how Paul experienced this I take comfort in the fact God allows these memories to keep me humble and to trust in his grace to be sufficient. I have peace that God has chosen to not remember such a past. Through my repentance for this, I have hope and forgiveness from The Lord as these things were done through ignorance rather than a willful rejection of God, as hard as that is for me to understand. **I did not know God through Christ. I knew of Him in an informed vain way that suited the identity I preferred for myself.** That identity was a man with deep thought, a man spiritual in his speech and one that felt he had a high sense of morality amongst a world without any. This identity is what many seek for themselves when they come to Christ. It is vain and without love of God but is rather self-centered. Many know of him in this deceived way so they can reference him or speak to his ways or quote his words. But hear me clearly, knowing him (Christ) truly is walking just as he did! Don't let anyone deceive you to think the words of Christ were not true. He said to follow him. He also said he is the truth, the way, and the life. So, we should follow him in truth, in his ways, and that is true life in the spirit. Doing this is our worship and our desire. If you are a child of God that is. God wants obedience to his ways more than any sacrifice you can think of giving. Be not deceived. The sacrifice that deceives many is the turning away from ways of living that did not work successfully in the world. By that I mean many would still drink, smoke, lie or sleep around if those ways had found success while in the world. Yet because many found it impossible to live comfortably in the world doing these things they turned to God for a more comfortable life. The love of God did not draw them. It was the abject failure of life that drew them to him. I am exposing this deception as many do not see it. It is why you see many able to not read his word or live according to it but clinging to the idea that they know God and receive his love. The flesh, even after claiming to follow Christ is raging out against the spirit that is trying to change the heart of that person. This is very challenging and will press each person in order that the very heart that is desperately wicked against God is changed **completely**. There is no shortcut here. It is the baptism by fire John referenced Jesus would do. This is rejected by the flesh and will always be. The flesh wants comfort of living here on earth. The Holy Spirit is interested in a genuine person from the inside and out. The flesh is more interested in being as genuine as it needs to be for the moment it benefits itself.

Consider the cost

The flesh wages war against the Holy Spirit for they are interested in two different things. The flesh is interested in pleasure and lifting itself up with the things of this world. The Holy Spirit desires righteousness and godliness and honor towards God through your life lived. For the children of God are new creatures on earth but not of the earth. This is not some cake walk for the weak. God has informed us exactly what will come from following his son. Many people hate this with passion, so it is rejected. Many desire all the benefits of having the sins we committed blotted out as though a life was not required for this. I found myself living like I forgot that a man gave his life for me. We have so many that have become numb to this statement because death in this generation is nothing more than something fun to do through a video game with others. Something interesting to watch on a Friday night. Death has become so watered down for our entertainment that by time it's our turn to experience it, the reality of it only shows up in that moment. So again, I say a man died for us! Consider what manner of man we are speaking of! **The man that died was the son of God. The creator of the universe**. Our very lives had a cost and through his love he paid for it. That's the good news that this was done for us considering we would never have been able to pay such a price. So, Jesus is telling us to consider the cost if we desire to follow him. What manner of thinking would try to receive such a priceless gift and think nothing is required of them after claiming to receive it. We didn't earn it or deserve it, the bare minimum we should do is respect it with our lives if we claim to receive it. Unfortunately, what appears to be happening is the treatment of it with contempt and arrogance. An actual preaching of freedom to indulge this flesh has surfaced despite Paul's warning to the Galatians to not use your freedom in Christ to indulge the flesh. Nothing in scripture creates this false comfort to live through the flesh as such, in fact all that is written speaks against such a way of thinking concerning the sacrifice of Jesus Christ. The very power of this flesh desires what it wants so bad that it will even use Jesus Christ name to get it. Those that are doing this are not considering the cost nor the penalty that will come from such a violation. Whenever you see someone claiming belief in Jesus and living casually in the world you see their lack of respect for him and his life. Doing and saying things that clearly show they have no regard for their words or actions. Love that person enough to explain the cost to them. They may not know of it but first ensure you know. Make no mistake, this will cost everyone their lives. If you live according to the flesh, you will reap death and death eternally. If you live according to the Spirit, you will reap life and life everlasting. To reap that life your life must be lived daily in the Spirit. Too many times those claiming the faith are looking to soothe themselves and others in sin. We are not called to soothe a sin. Rather we are called to love our brothers and sisters enough to rebuke them gently if they are caught in it. We are not doing anyone any favors by creating this false sense of it will be okay if you continue living in sin. The grace and mercies of God are not to be toyed with nor should a man tempt God. If you hear his voice to change your way of living, it is best you act upon that today! For who gave you tomorrow? Consider the cost of not treating his love with respect.

Warning against deeply deceiving spirits

There are many spirits that have gone out into the world. You are to test each one. Here is an example of how to test the spirit within yourself. I have presented this to many that claim the faith in Christ and have seen a consistent theme of rejection. Ironically, it concerns sin and not how you might think. When we think about sin, does your mind go to a place of we will always be in sin? Even if we walk with God and have his Holy Spirit? There are some that still cling to the idea that we will always be in sin. The fact this doesn't come across as blasphemous is astounding. The actual argument being made by many is that the blasphemy they see is having the mind of living sinless while in Christ. This is significant and blows me away with sorrow. This means many believe the power of the flesh is greater than the power of the Holy Spirit. What is it that this understanding desires me to believe? That regardless of being in Christ with the Holy Spirt, the flesh will still get its way within me? I wonder what scripture is read that gives anyone the idea they should reckon themselves alive to sin after receiving Christ. What I read is that in him I am dead to sin. So, what manner of being in Christ with his Holy Spirit makes me alive to sin again? Alive enough to it to continue to speak on it, in ways like "I will always sin"? This is what I reject by many professing Christians. This idea that this weak flesh is more powerful than the Holy Spirit that healed the sick, gave sight to the blind and brought the dead to life. Why are there so many clinging to the idea that we will always be prisoners to the very way of existing that Christ gave his life to redeem us from? It is because it is easier to believe in our weaknesses than to believe in Christ strength. It is not our strength that keeps us from sinning, rather it is the power of God that compels us to live in honor towards him. Instead of speaking in such a hypocritical way like we will always sin, how about we give the all-powerful God his true respect and honor. Yes honor, by letting the world know he has the power to keep us from sin. Many will not do this because it would truly ruffle even more feathers in and out of the church. As if what we believe is to be hidden to make others feel more comfortable. Ironically more comfortable in living apart from God. I seriously believe there is a lack of true understanding of Christ love existing within the church. We water down scriptures and don't address topics that touch on the ways of mankind. We dress up in this false form of love with soft words and so-called compassion. It's as if the priority is to hide the lack of care for the souls of others. For some I believe that's the case and for many its just a lack of understanding concerning the true reality of eternity. The power of the flesh has many still in shackles. Those shackles have many in fear to truly receive the very freedom Christ came to give and thereby they are ignorant of what that very freedom is from. When many read that we are free from the law, those who desire the world, and its ways receive that saying as I am free to do what I please because of the grace from God. Those who love God and desire his ways receive this truth as Gods' grace will keep me aware of what is not of him and in delight to do what is. I mean the flesh has so many convinced that it is humility to speak highly of their flesh and lowly of the Spirit. A clear agreement with the very nature of the flesh to always be present, even, and especially while with the Holy Spirit. I have never read any scripture that calls us to speak in such a way nor agree with such a teaching. Nonetheless this is a very popular ideology many share that claim to be believers in Christ Jesus. This shows the flesh waging war against the Spirit. It is beyond time that those that believe, believe boldly in our Lord. The nature of sin living is no longer a yoke around your neck. Stop putting it back on. Jesus gave his life that the yoke might be broken forever. To even speak of having a sinful nature puts Jesus back on the cross and shows a lack of understanding in whom the Father is.

Our calling

With all of this said, what should come to the surface is our very calling in Christ. This is important as it will keep you from corrupting yourself. Before I speak to these, remember to **first** seek The Kingdom of God **AND his righteousness.** This is very important for I just spoke to how the world has displayed a desire to present ways of God but without the right heart, so be careful. Be sure you do these things in honor of God and not yourself. I know we have heard the phrase our calling quite a bit within the church. It usually always involves someone speaking about a talent they have or a passion for an art or skill. You are not called to these things. These are simply your works that you enjoy. Our calling will always be to live on this planet as the salt. Meaning as the example of Christ which he gave us. How else will the world know transformation to be real? Our very lives are distinctively different from the world and how they live. With that said, here are some practical ways to walk out our calling. Start by owing no-one anything.

Payback your debts. Accrue none beforehand if possible. This is more than financial. If you owe an apology, give it quickly. If you have done something in error, confess it. Live without this worldly burden disguised as irrelevant. Pride resides within the one that renders such importance as meaningless. Also, if you lend money to someone do it without expecting to get it back. **Be truly generous**. Be not a burden to anyone in any way. If you cannot afford to give someone money without it becoming a burden in your life, then give them something else that will not become such. You either have it to give or you do not. Let your yes be yes and your no be no. With that said, resolve all disputes with peace. **Your opinion isn't required in life. Simply state facts of God**. Offer to those that seek them. You are not your own and anyone that wishes to receive truth can only do so through the Holy Spirit. Only He draws a person to God. So, don't make it your obligation to argue with a non-believer or convince anyone of the truth. **<u>You do that by how you live</u>**. The opinion is as quicksand, a fact is debated, but faith is an immovable stone. Remember you are a child of the same God the

Father that is to the Christ, and he is above all. Your responsibility is to him. For he is pure, so you are to be pure. We are to be Holy, for our Father is Holy. Carry yourself with the wisdom that Christ had. Operate with the clarity that your salvation was given as a gift by God. In ourselves we couldn't even accept it, let alone earn it. So, though we made the decision to believe in our hearts it was not truly through our own ability. So, we must endure this life in Christ as respect for it. Do not be deceived to think those that fall away or live as the world does will somehow be saved by a proclamation, concerning Jesus. Is not a spouse to live in a marriage with honor all the days of their life? Are they not to be faithful to that covenant until the day they die? Or are they simply covered by their wedding day vows, regardless of how they keep them during the duration of their marriage. This is not complicated, and God will not be mocked. Every confession concerning the son is vain if made without a life that aligns with it. It is our Lord that made this clear in **Matthew 15:8-12.**

Everyone proves their confession true by how they live. Everyone displays their hearts condition by their desires in this world. We are called to be the light on this planet to others. We came spiritually from the one true God of Israel in Christ. Do not sorrow the Holy Spirit by conducting yourself as if you are without knowledge. You have the truth and not many find it. This all is our calling. In this we show ourselves approved by the word and thus chosen by God.

Be not discouraged by hypocrites

My dear friends the road is narrow, it must be walked with focus. In this world you will hear things like you're a "goodie two shoes", or "you think you're holier than thou", or bluntly stated "you feel you are better than us". These are all things said to discourage you from living the way you are called to live. Those same people that speak like this to others who want to live in respect of Christ tolerate **liars, thieves**, **gossipers, and manipulators.** All the while these double-minded individuals display their hypocrisy when they are offended by those same people that live in those ways. This is made true the moment those ways conflict with their personal comfort of life.

Listen! Life will most certainly give you trouble. Yet true life in Christ will certainly give you peace through all that life presents. God doesn't need to remove the trouble to show his power all the time. He desires to remove our attachment of offence during it. For this shows his power made perfect in our weaknesses.

Our offence to the trouble shows a lack of faith in him.
It also shows an abundance of love or fear towards
the world. Neither leads us to the father. Many are
claiming Christ in hopes their life will not experience
trouble. The frustrations many experience that claim
Christ comes from their lack of understanding and
knowledge of him and the Father. The issue that's
existing is the idea that Christ came to earth, died on
a cross and rose again to grant earthly and worldly
comfort with worldly things. When many find this not
true from life experiences, they render the gospel null
and void for their lives. Their true heart's desires
become exposed, and you will see many that claim to
be believers but live for the peace the world gives.
The next new item purchased, the next new tv show,
the next vacation, the next new job, the next new
raise at work. This is the peace desired by many in
their lives. Not the peace from Christ but rather the

peace of circumstances going their way for a more comfortable life. For their peace is corruptible. Because this peace is based on material substances, typically government or worldly knowledge is looked to as the source to grant peace rather than living in it from Christ. They cannot comprehend true peace, for they have no source to it without Christ. So being of the world means seeking the peace this world offers and to go through the emotions of its failures to grant it. Be not confused, there has never been a generation that can attest to peace on earth from the world . This is the reason you hear this spoken of constantly by the world through worldly gain. They clamor for it and desire to create this deceiving peace on earth. Make no mistake about it, it is written; they will receive the only form of peace the world gives when it comes. When it does come to the world, it will be of the devil and will be masked as a form of good.

Be not deceived, this peace the world will refer to is not from God. It is rather the one that wants to dismiss the truth in Christ to receive their truth which is simply a lie. That selfish false truth is that there are several ways to God, and that sin is not what God says it is but subjective, or rather justifiable dependent on the situation. It will celebrate those that delight in these things and wish for you to be open to their form of understanding and living. Corruption runs wild in the world, run not with them, rather run against them. As in the opposite of their passions. "Let us lay aside every **weight, and sin** which so easily shows up in us and let us run with patience the race set before us". Hebrews 12:1

Submit yourself mentally

To **struggle** is to truly know life and secretly it develops **humility.** Make no mistake about this though, you can struggle in life and not develop humility. When I say struggle, I refer to the awareness all must have of the weakness the flesh has. The fickleness of the mind. Until a person recognizes this about themselves, they can only exist with pride. This is why God is not near the prideful. The prideful say in their hearts I don't need God and I can take care of everything on my own. This person does not understand their ultimate weakness. We all have this, which is why Christ, and the Holy Spirit are so important. For it is written that the heart is more deceptive than all other things. How obvious it is that the heart is the very thing the world desires many to follow. How do you convince someone who has decided in their heart they can figure out all their issues on their own? If this is their position concerning life, how great is their ignorance concerning their soul? That is the heart that does not desire God.

Now many hear the word heart, and it can be confusing. **So, whenever you hear the word heart understand it means the conviction a person lives by. How a person thinks about all things with conviction to live them outwardly.** This exposes the deception many have used to dismiss their actions that don't align with the word of God. That deception used is a common statement popularized by claimers of the faith. That statement is ironically "God knows my heart". This is only stated when someone doesn't uphold what the word of God says. The reason it's used may surprise those that use it. I will speak to why I once used this deceiving statement and what God revealed to me about it once he brought me from the darkness of its deception. The reason I used this statement and believe whole heartedly many are using it also is because it helps our conscience feel connected to God despite actions that reject him. Now here is what God revealed to me years ago concerning this. **Many use this statement when they don't live according to my words because they don't associate their living, and their behaviors as a reflection of knowing me.** They are deceived and have a vain belief towards my son just as you did Philip. That's what I heard from God concerning this. This was groundbreaking for me! Seriously life altering for I could not dispute any of this as I suddenly was made very aware that this was true. How could I not? I mean, Jesus stated **IF** you love me, you will keep my commandments. Ephesians 2:8-10 tells me we were saved **for** good works. So how can anyone dismiss the necessity of our lives to be reflections of God as our love towards him or lack thereof. It is because deception has creeped into the assembly of claimers.

Deception is the leader of this world. Many wear the mask of it, while it smiles in delight of its many ways. Exercising all its gifts and practicing all its arts. This is sorrowful, and once you see the conflict in this world that rages against God you will find that Solomon was correct when he said all is vanity. Think clearly and directly upon your soul. **You** are the one in control of your thoughts by way of free will that God grants us all. The teacher of them must be Christ as the author is God. **Submit your thoughts to them**. They will help with what you ought to say and do. The world says to replace your negative thoughts with positive ones, yet if both are from the world they still lead to **death.** Be not deceived by a positive worldly thought that has nothing to do with Christ but focuses on success or gain. This is deceiving **deathly wisdom**. The soul must be prioritized. Don't we understand that what helps the soul helps the flesh also? We are aware that what we put our mind to, displays our desires. So, replace all thoughts with the words of God which are true and are life, and our desires will be transformed into the will of Yahweh (God). Then our thoughts will be true and produce light from our Lord.

The Kingdom <u>AND</u> his righteousness are required

Remember the Kingdom of God is within and all around us! We cannot see it or perceive it because our eyes are on the world and its self-created things. I remember when I was made aware of the nature of my mind and being renewed by the word of God I started to see differently. The trees and the sky, the moon and the sun were all now thought upon as the creation of God. Sounds loopy I know but think about this. We wake up every day and are so used to a burning ball of fire in the sky that contributes to the life on this planet. As a child we would have so many questions and be in awe of the very common things we know so much about now. Yet these created living sources came from the one true God. They are intended to show proof of his existence to us. The kingdom is everything he created, and we are to be in awe of it all. Now pagans started worshipping those created things by God instead of God. Which shows mankind needed Christ deeply. We have no idea of the way, the truth, or the life we should live without him. To understand the kingdom of God is to understand the power of God as supreme. To be in acknowledgement of his presence. We are to seek this but **also** his righteousness. Once many have perceived the Kingdom of God, they find that sufficient alone for their lives. This cannot save anyone for it is written that even the demons believe and yet they tremble at the mention of the Son. It is his righteousness that we must seek that shows our love for him.

This is not a faith based on emotions and feelings. Since much of our understandings stem from emotions and feelings, many seek God with those things alone. You can clearly see this being done by many as I once did also. This is because when we hear seek the Kingdom of God, we look to have an emotional attachment to him through our experiences. That is what coming to Christ with all your heart is mistaken for many times. Be not confused by this statement. The emotional state of a person can draw them in their need for God, but this is why God doesn't tell us to simply seek his Kingdom alone. We are also informed that the heart is more deceiving than all other things, and desperately wicked. So, we know a person can have an emotional experience one day and the very next day act as if that very moment never happened. This explains why God states to seek his righteousness also. For seeking his righteousness is a daily pursuit. Only those that truly believe in what they proclaimed concerning Jesus commit their lives to those words. Those words we used were that we believe that Jesus is the son of God. So, though an emotional connection can be what draws a person, the pursuit of righteousness through Christ is not an emotional aspect or one based on feelings. This is very much a mentality of conviction on how you live your life. The greatest commandment is to seek God with all your heart, mind, soul, and strength. The emotional experience does not have to be rejected; it just cannot stand alone. I have found many are operating with one or the other. Rarely all, yet I believe all are needed to truly experience God in every way while on earth. It is a commandment from our Lord. A person with just Kingdom knowledge and a lack of righteousness, will display that knowledge in many forms of unstable emotions and feelings. A person with emotional attachment to the word alone and no Kingdom knowledge displays this typically with a lack of biblical understanding. Both can be damaging to others and themselves as it is not the full view of God. Deception can easily creep in at this stage, so it is very important to seek both the Kingdom of God and his righteousness. A classic modern-day case of this is the view many have on homosexuality. There are many that claim to be seeking God through Jesus

Christ that practice this lifestyle. The reason they can do this and why many are agreeing with their desire to do so is because many get caught up on the Kingdom of God alone. The seeking of his righteousness is dismissed. This is how a person can live deceived, thinking they can have a relationship with God while living in a sinful way his word speaks against. There is really no difference concerning the sin per se. For there are liars, cheaters, those in fits of rage and vain people that claim to follow Christ. Again, it is because seeking righteousness in God is neglected and many believe his Kingdom is all the knowledge they need. The truth is simple here. Having one alone will not be sufficient before Christ. There must be a seeking of his Kingdom and his righteousness also. Be aware that Jesus speaks to those who only sought his Kingdom alone and not his righteousness. In Revelations 7:21-23, Jesus informs those who did many works in his name that he never knew them. He informs them that they were workers of lawlessness not because of the things they did in his name, but rather the fruit they displayed in their lives towards others, specifically those they thought less of. Seek his righteousness I say again. He is looking for a life that bears good fruit to all people. Not just people you have something in common with or people that like you. Not just people who say they are Christians and have jobs or positions within their local church. No, all people, especially your enemies. This is why his righteousness is key, because in his righteousness the standard is Christ himself and that is what he did. So, the church that he seeks are not so much those that call themselves Christians but rather people who are Christians everywhere they go and with everyone they interact with. Those who stand for his word and against all manners of sin within themselves first, and in the world. Those are his true followers, and they

are not in conflict with him or themselves.

(shlishi) שְ.לְ.יִשׁ.י

<u>Religious deception</u>

John 8:32 **And ye shall know the truth, and the truth**

shall make you free.

The first part of this scripture is key. Many want the

truth and many want freedom, but what about the

initial verse leading to these things. For the verse

listed starts with the word "**<u>And</u>**" which means there

was something spoken prior to this statement that is

important. Extremely important in fact. That extremely

important statement is this. "If you abide in My word, you are My disciples indeed. There's the prerequisite. "If" you abide in his word. The word abide is a verb. **Meaning this isn't about what I call myself or a feeling for a season, but rather a state of existence that produces a life that aligns with his word**.

Let no man nor woman tell you to follow any structure of religion. For Christ brought "truth" not religion. There was a time that telling you to follow Christianity was what would be best, but the Christianity of the **western world** primarily has been corrupted. Unfortunately following it can lead to the same hell that non-believers and those of other religious beliefs will see because it follows **itself <u>not</u> Christ**. I'm sure this is confusing and that has been by design by the enemy.

Honestly, the church opened the door for this by creating different divisions within itself. Debating over doctrines and allowing that spirit of division into a body that we were told not to allow. 1 Corinthians 1:10 clearly states this; I appeal to you, brothers, and sisters, in the name of our Lord Jesus Christ, that all of you **agree** with one another in what you **say** and that there be **no** divisions **among** you, but that **you** be perfectly united in **mind and thought.** It is said if you wish to kill the body take out the head. The mind per se. This has been done to those who have not desired true understanding in Christ. You will find sermons on doctrines that are not even in the word of God. You have the **prosperity gospel,** then you have the "**you are a god gospel**", you have the **sow this specific amount of money for a breakthrough gospel**, the **speak into existence gospel,** and many others alike these roaming around

85

wearing sheep clothing as if this were the teachings of Yeshua. Ironically each one of these Satanic gospels where exposed when Satan tempted Jesus. Look no further than the temptations Satan presented to Jesus, and you will find each one he presented to Yeshua as the teachings many false teachers teach for Christians to receive. I mean you can't make this up. It is all written for us to learn from and understand his deceiving voice. Yet many dance and rejoice when what Satan presented to Jesus is presented to us. This shows our desire is for the world and not God. This unfortunately has been strategic by Satan. Some may wonder why God would allow such corruption to even come within the church. The deception many fall into with such a question is the idea that Satan can do something to defeat God. **The only thing these Satanic teachings within the church do is expose the hearts of those that prefer them.** Those that delight themselves in the Lord are given a Holy Spirit of discernment that reveals all truth to them. This thereby separates the true Church of Christ from those who prefer the Satanic version created to serve themselves.

I tell you what the western world's Christianity is. The structure not the gospel. For the bible is without error. Those that claim to believe in it and follow that structure rarely read it. So, the religion was derived from the Roman Catholic church. That church and power came from pagan backgrounds masked in honoring Christ. The attempt that was successful at least in part to create a mixed version of how to follow Christ was to integrate practices that were never amongst Jewish customs let alone the people that followed Christ. For many of the Jewish customs were exposed as vain by Christ. Ponder that for a second. Yeshua came and exposed the religious teachers' hearts and many of their vain customs. Yet many think he would welcome the pagan customs indoctrinated by those of gentile descent because they claim to honor him with them. This is not confusing; Of course, he wouldn't!

To provide clarity about a pagan. Understand this is someone who indulges in worldly delights and material possessions; someone who revels in sensual pleasures. Many times, opting to perform worship to materials or things in nature rather than to God the creator of such things. This new Christianity uses greed and manipulation to alter your mind around things of the world. It uses the mind of Satan to glorify the things of this world through prayer for them, or the use of your words to manifest them. It agrees with the change of the Sabbath day that was done by the Catholic church to honor the day with worship that they feel better suits the life of this world. It believes that the things of this world are what The Holy Spirit grants instead of the things of Heaven.

Now, this is loaded I know. **This is important to know but it's even _more_ important to point out what the true gospel and faith is, rather than what deception has tried to sow within it.**

The true church is separated

Many have been turned away from Christianity because of these sorts of manipulative teachings. For even those lost in the world can see something doesn't add up when hearing them. Unfortunately, many that claim Christ are usually the ones that welcome these false doctrines. Clearly this reveals what their true desires are! Be not deceived, this is not following Christ!! These are not the teachings of Christ, and because they speak his name and blaspheme the Holy Spirit with these ways, their judgment shall be great, as it is written. So, allow me to clarify through the guidance of the Holy Spirit what following Christ is. It is first reading your Bible for yourself and asking God to help you see the changes needed in your life. When you do that, you will see a man in Jesus Christ that denied his very flesh. He denied any desires of this world and all things that come from it such as, lust, selfishness, and pride. Take every word he spoke and apply it to your life. This must be done daily with intentional focus. The Holy Spirit will bring a truly open heart to a place of repentance as your life will be exposed as corrupt without God. Once your true repentance has taken place, God will begin molding your life into his sons, with rebukes and correction. This will keep you humble as you will see clearly you cannot do this without the Holy Spirit. This is the love God will show everyone that desires him. Those that love Christ, prove their love with daily thought and application of his words. Every word spoken and every action taken has a conscious consideration of him. The lie is that we cannot do this in this flesh. This lie proves hypocritical as we can clearly point to ways of life that we live considering **ourselves** first without any issue at all. Yet when it comes to following Christ, many are relying on the weakness of this flesh to excuse our falling or sinning against God. It is through that very weakness of this flesh that the power of God is made perfect as it is written. This tells me that when we submit to Christ completely the very grace many try to manipulate for sin or to excuse sin is the opposite. The grace of God is now here through his Holy Spirit to help us walk just as his son did. It is not to excuse sins after coming to the truth in Christ. For it is written in Hebrews 10:26 that there is no more sacrifice for sin if we deliberately continue in sin after coming to the knowledge of the truth. Put it this way, if you have enough awareness to speak about the grace of God when it comes to you doing what you know is sin, then you are not using your knowledge of the truth for good. Rather you are using it as a blanket to excuse yourself. Those that truly love the Lord are seeking his grace to live according to his word, not the opposite. Self-centeredness and self-desire remain the forbidden fruits that mankind loves the taste of. It still has its appeal of wisdom and encompasses the very knowledge of good and evil.

The deception of self-desire remains the most difficult aspect to remove and receive as needing to be removed for mankind. **It is the most difficult because the true desire for our own lives is to not remove it at all, if we are honest with ourselves.** I believe that Satan desired to make every form of religion through this. **Everyone's desire is to serve**

themselves. Everyone desires a god that will serve them. Yet everyone in Christ must consider the nature of dying to themselves daily. In Christ we learn that the object of focus is to remove our selfish desire by dying to it daily. **The religious deception that has the world imprisoned is the idea that you can keep self-desire as long as you claim to be honoring God**. This has simply produced a deep searing of consciousness in people. Those of the faith see this as the very area that must be denied daily for it is the teaching of our Lord. Thus, this separates the true church of Christ, and no manner of false gospels which aren't gospels at all can snatch them out of his hand.

The deceiving religion of self

There is a consistent theme when one considers all religions. We clearly find that they were created by men who looked within to glorify themselves. They disregarded others in their quest. Yet others follow in hopes to do the same. They do not understand the requirement for a sacrifice to atone for their sins. Since the faith of self-desire drives and motivates their lives, the idea of someone else being required to make them right with God is ridiculous. Pride drives the religions of this world. There even is a religion of atheism that speaks openly that the human and its mind is sufficient alone. As for the other religions they simply have their own customs and gods created that make you right through your works. The draw to many is to have the life one desires here on earth and a promise after it. Many even use the draw of pleasing God as the reward. This further shows that one can live deeply deceived by self-desire.

The main reason self-desire motivates these religions is because none of these religions have a **man** that was and is the living proof of God the Father with the Holy Spirit operating within him. None have a man that suffered death only to rise again. None have a man that had miracles witnessed from his hand, and his words. Yeshua The Christ was this man though. When you read what he said you see he had no desire for fame from these things. No desire for earthly glorification from these things but rather pointed everyone back to The Father in Heaven. Understand what he is saying here in John 5:30. I can of **my own self do nothing**: as I hear, I judge: and my judgment is just; because I seek not mine own will, but the will of the Father which hath sent me. How many are speaking this way in this generation? How many have spoken this way ever? If we can be honest with ourselves, we understand that our natural way of talking is the opposite of this. The false doctrines of self-gratification mentioned above actually promote the opposite of what the Christ states here. The man Yeshua taught us to deny ourselves. The teachings of today speak of welcoming things to yourself. As you can see those are two different teachings. This proves' him to be true. This amongst the testimony of John the Baptist shows that the anointed one from God was upon us. He was not interested in finding some comfort of life here on earth but having God in Him while here. Religious deception will not allow you to receive this. It is interested in **you** above God. Everything it presents is in alignment with helping you be the best **you.** It is very challenging to speak against this because who doesn't want to be encouraged and spoken into with positive words of affirmation. Here is the subtle wrinkle the evil one slips in when doing such a thing. He attempts to remove God from the equation. For example, if I tell someone every morning you wake up to go to the bathroom and look in the mirror and say I am great, I am blessed, I am good, I am positive, I am successful, I choose to love others today, I am smart, etc. etc....No one would challenge that practice as being a bad idea. Notice the subtlety within the I am. We take who God is and replace him with ourselves. For he is the I AM. He is the only one that can make statements like such for he was not created by anyone. When we use "I am" concerning ourselves to align with whatever character we desire, its important we insert God's character but also that God is the focus. God doesn't align with any character we desire for ourselves **alone**. He is love and has the character of love and true Holy love is not self centered. Satan does not want your words to submit to God, but rather to **yourself**. The evil one knows you do not have to call yourself a Satanist to align with him, he is more interested in you worshipping yourself. For this is the true worship of Satan but I will digress.

Anytime you speak an, "I am" statement, show him you are submitted to Christ and make sure your statement is in Christ. For your life is not your own, meaning you cannot speak about yourself apart from Christ unless you are apart from Christ. One that submits to Christ as Lord speaks in a manner that honors him above themselves. So, you should say I am positive in Christ, I am blessed in Christ, I am successful in Christ, I choose to love others today in Christ. Yes, in Christ alone. For outside of him we are nothing more than desperately wicked and selfish in our desires.

In Christ, you find that your works are a **by-product** of your true faith in the man Yeshua. For in him the Holy Spirit dwelt, and through your true belief in him it will dwell in you also. This will allow your deeds to be we walked for several hours. I was informed by my uncle that we will be picking up more guys who have been waiting for him. We reached our destination. There were over 15 people waiting, including families and kids. We started our journey with our guide, which is my uncle, who had very little patience for crying kids. He made it very clear to us that we had to control our kids and keep the noise down, especially when we arrived at the camp where the soldiers were stationed at the top of the mountain. We traveled through the valley, which was close to the camp (of the enemy). That was the only safe way to get through. Our guide kept telling us to keep quiet and to stay together throughout the journey. He placed a lot of fear in all of us, but then again, he was the expert, and he knew the situation better than we did.

We started our journey. I was one of the people who stayed in the rear, helping a family who had younger kids. Our dirt road was surrounded by a lot of big trees. These trees gave us shade and made the trip a little easier. In fact, we enjoyed eating a lot of wild fruits as we traveled on our journey. We arrived at yet, another village where we spent a few hours and got plenty of rest. At midnight, the guide came and gathered all of us. He explained to us what we needed to do as we crossed to our next point, we had to go through this deep valley, and this valley is surrounded by an Iraqi camp at the top of the hill. We can only cross in the night during the day time. This will be our only way out. Keep in mind that if we get caught, that will be our end. "We will do this, one group at a time". He also advised us that the family with kids is to make sure that they are asleep and have their hand on their mouth in case they cry to keep them quiet. As we got closer to the valley that would take us to the Kurdish fighters, of us, and there were other people who were waiting to be picked up. We set out on a narrow dirt road and traveled through some very rough mountain terrain. We continued to follow the path through a valley and on the edge of a small river that flows through this valley. I believe we walked for at least three to four hours before we even sat down and took a break. My uncle kept me on the run. I kept saying to myself, "This man is very strong. How is he able to walk for such a long time without breaking a sweat?" He must be, at least, in his late fifties. He looked old but strong. The living situation for these comrades was very hard. They are always on the run and always in fear of the enemy, they live off of the land, and they travel from one village to another village carrying their belongings and their guns. I kindly asked him him for food and time to rest for a bit, but all he had was some dry bread and water, which was more than enough to satisfy our need for food and water. As we got close to a small village, I was really excited knowing that we were going to have a nice hot meal. We arrived at the village, and had a nice warm meal and water that was offered to us by one of the villagers. Best meal in a long time, and now we needed to rest. I was hoping my uncle will allow us to stay for the night. After all, we are exhausted, or rather, I am exhausted. I was in desperate need for some sleep. My uncle told me we would be spending the night at the village with top-notch hospitality. They took excellent care of us, and I made sure to keep my stomach full.

After a long walk, I had no problem falling asleep and slept throughout the night. On the following day, right at dawn, we had breakfast and hot tea. We were able to get some extra bread for the road. I felt that I was ready to continue the journey, so we left the village. With an unknown destination, done from the **right heart.** Not in complete disregard of the heart as the world does. It is said by the world to do the works that make you **feel** better. This is deception and it is self-seeking. A person is literally making it clear that the deed done was for themselves when they say such a thing. Doing right is not a potion to soothe whatever stress you have or conflict you have in who you are. Abandon this religion of self and humble yourself to the throne of God. Who else has given everything blameless and pure to save such a soul that was everything but?

I share all of this in hopes no-one might fall as I have. Seeking God with the wrong heart and motivated by self-centered desires.

The true teachings of Jesus

The Christ said in **Matthew 6:25** "I tell you, **do not worry** about **your life,** what you will **eat or drink**; or about **your body**, what you **will wear**. Is not life more than food, and the body more than clothes"? So, as you can see there is no way this teaching be from the world. No way this teacher is of the same Christianity we see dominating the western world. Other religions also say consider these things and how they shall be attained. Understand what **Hebrews 10:34** is truly saying here. "**Our citizenship is in heaven, and from it, we await a Savior, the Lord Jesus Christ**". Also, here in **Philippians 3:20. If we love, follow, and serve Christ, wherever we live in this world, we know we belong somewhere else.** How many people that say they are Christian believe this? How many of us truly feel to die is to gain as it means being with God? I pose these questions because it is at the heart of our faith. Such a statement is not requiring you to consider something uncommon to God like taking your own life or acting in a way that is erratic or unstable because of it. Rather a strong understanding that the God in Yeshua the Christ **never claimed** to present an **easy life** to anyone. Jesus did not have a place to lay his own head. He was also an innocent man sentenced to death. His followers were martyred and jailed. Think about this. **God willfully allowed these men and women to endure this, let alone his own son. He did not allow this in vain, but that we might learn how to walk with him as Jesus did and his devout followers did. Yet many believe 2000 years later that God has changed, so we could have our minds on the world's possessions, comfort of living and money.** To listen to such preaching's and teachings shows a true hatred for the gospel. **To even suggest God has a focus for your life that wants you to prosper financially so you can enjoy the materialistic things in this world, would be**

contradictory to everything in the Bible. Many desire to believe in God with the emphasis on him providing finances, food, clothing of their choice and living that suits their desire. Isn't it interesting that in a country that has churches on each corner has no one there hungry or naked? Those that are, usually are outside the church building. It is clear these desires cannot be satisfied as many cannot even see that God has already taken care of it in their lives. This is about self-centeredness and the love of the world. The sorrow of knowing many will give their whole mind and hearts to these things when God simply stated to seek him first and he would add them to you. You would think he said he would withhold them from you considering how many people sell their souls to the devil for these things. It is quite simply a blasphemous understanding and nothing more than the works of Satan to corrupt what is true. Is this really that hard to see? Truth is, it isn't desired to be received by many. It is obvious why the selfish gospel, which isn't a gospel at all is more preferred. The true gospel doesn't consider your worldly desires. It tells you to deny them and make the desire God and God alone. The teachings of Jesus tell us clearly to deny these worldly things from within. Yet I guess many believe that because he has given his life, he wants you to focus on them now. Do we really believe that? Clearly this world is only concerned about seeking the desires of oneself only. In broad daylight we see that the light is hated, and darkness is desired. Every single person on this planet that has ever lived proves the Bible true by the very way of thinking and living that exists. A young person follows the same pattern shown to them in the world and expects different results. They grow older and give birth to their own children and show them the same patterns that corrupted them, and that child grows up and follows the same disfunction expecting different results. This sorrowful pattern is literally the world's generation after generation. Everyone can clearly see that the pattern is corrupt but cannot see the truth to turn from it because they love corruption and have found enjoyment within it.

1 John 2:15 Do not love the world or anything in the world. If anyone loves the world, love for the father is not in them.

Now the Christ also brought two commandments. Not unlike the 10 our father gave Moses. Rather the essence of all 10. The 2 commandments Jesus referenced was to love God with all your heart, with all your soul, and with all your mind. His next commandment was to love your neighbor as yourself. So, let's examine these two.

Loving God with all of you is key. You cannot truly love anyone else if you do not have the love of The Father in place initially. Also, as listed above, it is written that if you love the world or the things in the world, the love of the Father is not in that person. So, examine yourself! Claiming to love God while indulging in the things of this world or believing the lies in it is proof that your love for him is not genuine. Be not deceived, it is not! Essentially loving your neighbor as yourself is all contingent on how you love yourself. If you treat yourself badly then treating others badly will be your norm. Those who love God with all their mind, body and soul will automatically create a selflessness within themselves. Thereby loving your neighbor will be common practice. So, to conclude, Jesus Christ has given us the blueprint to follow. Love God with all of yourself. This will create selflessness from within and that is the necessary component to love others.

The true gospel of Yeshua (Jesus) Christ is one that offends many when spoken correctly. The word of God is not of this world, though it is in those that reside here that believe God sent his son to bring it and shed his blood for it. The world rejected him and knew him not and in effect welcomed the judgment that comes from such a rejection.

It is important to depart from this world. You would not catch a ride with someone who told you they were on their way to rob a bank unless you wanted some parts of that activity enough to disregard any potential consequences from it. Consider your walk just the same. If you wish to be of this world, then you are telling God you desire to enjoy the ways of this world. You desire it more than any regard towards the judgment promised to it. Whether you respect the judgment or not, you are saying that the way God made for us to come back to him through his son is not needed for your existence. When you follow another belief, you are saying all these things, and that you enjoy what the world has to offer you above what you feel God can offer. If you say you are Christian, and you are receiving teachings that contradict the ones of Christ, you tell God I prefer the man or woman telling me these ways to profit here on earth. I prefer the wisdom of death rather than the wisdom of life. **Be not deceived you are telling God these things from how you live**. So many times, we wish to conceal our deepest truths to live with a false sense of comfort in this world. Many are doing this rather than dealing with the true root of a matter. I've found that this is done to prevent the real possibility of us coming to terms with what we are and what we believe. From my personal experience, I tell you the truth. You should have that epiphany of these things about yourself as soon as possible. It is better done now than for your breath to leave you and it be too late.

What does God want from us?

You will not offend God by saying I don't know you, God. He already knows if you don't. He wants humility. He wants a pure and true relationship with us where we are honest about our motives and desires inwardly to him. He wants to alter our motives, so they align with his will. When we conceal them, we say I'd rather not care to know your will, God. I wish for you to sign off on my will, and if you don't my disappointment, my discouragement, and anger towards you should be understood. That's the arrogance we carry towards God. When we finally know Him, we see the religious deception we have been under. For this is true. There are many spirits in this world. The word of God says to test them, test every single one of them to see if it is from God. The spirit of deception is what confounds the world. It operates in many forms. Some claim Christ and have no love for him or his teachings. Some don't believe Christ was the son of God at all but claim to know God. Then you have those that claim another faith belief system apart from Christ. Then you have those that don't believe God even exist. That spirit delights in darkness and desires no life or light to its understanding. As you can see there are many ways of deception. All these spirits are from the wicked one that is a deceiver, and the word says he has deceived the whole world. Departing from this world is essential. Again, departing from this world mentally is key. Understand you are adopted by God to be his child if you choose to believe in his son. If you choose deception and believe there is a truth elsewhere for you, or feel life is easier without Christ then understand the cost. For Christ informed those that wish to follow him to consider the cost in doing so prior as well. So, with both choices, I suggest you consider the cost as you should. My children, my brothers, and sisters in Christ. Drink from the words of Christ and there shall be no-more thirst in life for life will be attained. Do not over-complicate your existence here. The world desires to do that for you. Sin accomplishes it. You will have thoughts in your mind of course, but you will also have thoughts presented to you by others. These will occur through television viewing, social media interactions, direct interactions with family or friends, or individuals you may encounter through school or work. Everyone has their views. You must learn of Christ to know God and to do that you must first seek the Kingdom of God and his righteousness! Again, the Kingdom of God is within your midst. This was taught by the Christ. The chosen and anointed one by the incorruptible light that is Father of the universe. My children and my friends you must read the Bible! Read Proverbs and Psalms for practical wisdom. Read the words from Christ for righteousness. Read the word of the Prophets to see how those God chose to free from slavery, rebelled against him and the punishments they received because of it. Read about Gods compassion he had for them to return to him after if they repented. Read! Read why a sacrifice was necessary and when God informed his people of its coming. Learn about those that believed in him and carried the gospel of Jesus to the world. Then read how God plans to bring an end to this world and make all things new again. Study to find yourselves approved by God and his ways. Seek who you follow.

Educate yourself on him. This will expose the true condition of mankind and yourself. Once you believe that you are a sinner and understand that only God can remove that; then and only then will you be interested in what he sent for that to be possible.

Deception can be broken

Man changed his purpose and the purpose of the world with sin. Essentially desiring it for himself in any manner he chooses. **He designed a structure for himself and those that would come after to glorify themselves.** Whether it be a feeling of accomplishment, a desire to be wise, a lust for flesh and worldly pleasures, or pride. All is deception and all of it is vanity. Seek and follow Christ, he brought truth and accomplished what The Father's will was without interjecting his own. Our call is to simply do the same. The simple but complex gift of salvation is to live out the very love that was shown to us. The simple yet very complex gift of grace from God is to give it to others. The simple but extremely complex forgiveness shown through his mercy is required of us whom believe, to give to others. How can we even remotely claim to not understand such a thing? We are the beneficiaries of a gift and a love we never earned. Let this be understood. Our very religion, which is a word to describe a set of beliefs that one lives by is this indeed. Be not deceived by those who say things such as I'm spiritual but not religious, in other words, they mean, my mouth speaks of spiritual things but don't expect my life to reflect it. This is religious deception. The desire is to distance themselves from the corruption of the church and in doing so they create a new form of corruption. This is done instead of investing truly their time into the word of God for themselves so that they understand truly what has been written. Instead, more confusion is sown into the world concerning the faith of those who do not know. Regardless know this, that I am living proof that deception can be broken after thinking I knew God while living sexually immoral and as a liar. By God's grace, integrity and honor are my desires and to speak to all who will hear about the freedom from sin through Jesus Christ. I tell you the truth, this deception of religion cannot be broken without first being honest with God. **The honesty God seeks for this deception to be broken is one that professes you never knew him.** Paul, once Saul is proof that deception can be broken after thinking he knew God while persecuting and killing Christians. By God's grace he would bring the gospel of Jesus Christ to the gentiles. King David is proof that deception can be broken after falling into sexual desire and immorality he repented and sought God with all his heart. Peter is proof that deception can be broken after having zeal and courage just to find that fear and self-preservation births cowardness. By God's grace he found his zeal and courage through repentance to bring the gospel to the Jews. I could go on, but I believe you understand the point. That point is to think not too highly of yourself so that you cannot be deceived. Above that, think not too highly of deception to think you cannot be freed from it with the truth. Truth is, God provides proof of himself to all who desire to receive it. Truth is, God desires to be known by who he is, not by who we desire him to be. I hope that this is received and helps someone understand the significance of this deception. Jesus stated this in **John 17:3 And this is eternal life, that they may know You, the only true God, and Jesus Christ whom You have sent.**

Our Lord is saying that knowing God is eternal life! Yet if we cannot admit we don't know him, we resist him and reject eternal life**. This remains the hardest admission to make from both the world and those in the church.** It is because they have believed the lie. The lie for the world is that they can be a good person through their own efforts, even though those efforts fail they trust in themselves. The lie the claimers of the faith have believed is that God is understanding of their sins. That he has them covered once they have claimed to believe in Christ. So, for those who truly desire to know him we must understand that knowing him is living our lives just as our Lord did.

1 John 2:4-6 sums it up like this and it is a perfect closing to this chapter.

If someone claims, "I know him well!" but doesn't keep his commandments, he's obviously a liar. His life doesn't match his words. But the one who keeps God's word is the person in whom we see God's mature love. This is the only way to be sure we're in God. Anyone who claims to be intimate with God ought to live the same kind of life Jesus lived.

Be not deceived! Your very life and how you live it proves what you believe! Let no one tell you anything different.

Shalom-Peace

ר ֵב ֨יע ֗י (revi'i)

<u>False Love Faith</u>

<u>1 John 4:8-But anyone who does not love does not know God, for God is love</u>

So much of what many neglect in reading this verse results in deception. Yes, God is love. Do people truly know what the love of God is? It is spoken of so much in this generation that you clearly see many believe God's love is the accepting of their choices. The openness to all lifestyles and acceptance of all cultures. **This shows that man believes the love of God is one that does not correct them.** One that does not say no. So, in this they show that there is no understanding of who God is. God is love, so there is no understanding of true love either. The God they are speaking of is the God of deception and confusion. The God they are referencing when claiming their way of living to be love or accepted by God is the God of this world. The one that hates them actually and considers them irrelevant. So, this God that wants everyone to live and act out the very desires of their hearts and accept all that wish to do the same, will never correct them. **For it is Satan.** The one true living God and Father corrects those he loves. In fact, he rebukes those he loves because that's what love does. It loves a person more than their comfort of living; it loves a person more than some self-centered fear of disrupting a bond. It loves a person's soul more than their flesh. It considers their soul above all things. This is the love of God. This is the love we are called to show to others. Not the version we have learned from the world, which is not love at all. Rather it is a form of hatred for another wrapped in self-centeredness. Masking itself as accepting and caring for the well-being of others while truly indifferent towards the souls they support. This must be received or the very foundation of knowing God will always be distorted. We will always try to understand God and his love through the lens of our personal experiences or our own personal efforts. Never considering his son, nor what he did through him. At best we will hear about Jesus dying on a cross as another good story mixed in with the many, we grew up hearing. We will become so numb to the reality of that historical event that it will be met with such contentment that even while claiming to be a believer you will find yourself with a chuckle or a scoff at the very account. This is happening clearly today amongst this generation that see's Jesus' death and resurrection as nothing more than a story to go along with Santa Claus coming down a chimney with gifts for them and the Easter bunny dropping colorful eggs for children. Now though we understand none of that to be real we still allow our children to be introduced to such pagan wickedness. So, let's travel back in time to where we all started our form of understanding, for this is just a microcosm of a greater disfunction.

Our desires hate correction

At some point in life, most people found **correction** a bad thing. Seeing as most of us grew up in an environment that had someone telling us no or correcting us we must examine. Our response to this was always based around the idea that what we desire is being restricted. Never really viewing the person doing the correction as a form of love because we loved our desires more. This explains why our view of God's love is distorted. The person that did this correction was typically our parents to start in life. In doing the correction many parents may have lost their temper or may have lived a life that was difficult for us to respect. So, at a young age we associated love separate from correction. When we considered how the information concerning our actions was delivered, we looked for what could justify our rebellion against it. Then we examined the ways and lives of our parents to discredit the information. When we examined our parents' lives and saw what didn't align, we used that as our fuel to discredit them. The root of our rebellion was a **lack of respect** for the one who informed us to not do a thing we **wanted** to do.

This is where we all learned the idea of love. So, if we grew up with sadness, fear, or anger at the form of love our parents displayed to us, we associate it without even knowing it to God. This may be true, but if we are honest, the root of love we comprehended at a young age was, "**does this person agree with what I want to do**". This was always proven true by how important the voices of our friends were. It didn't matter what mom or dad said concerning a matter. What mattered to us was what our friends had to say. Typically, if not completely and almost certainly, our friends were into the same things we were. We respected their input and views and that was the foundation our understanding had concerning the right thing to do. For our friends were into the same things as we were, so obviously they were not going to correct us. Yet we felt they cared for us because we didn't associate love with correction. In fact, we started a pattern of faith in believing love came without correction. Many are living with this understanding, with the false love faith that has no correction within it. This is how many choose to hear God as only a yes man to their desires. This is how many choose to pray about matters in their lives. There is a belief that God only loves us in an accepting manner of what we want. So now we have a fuel of emotion that only seeks God for the fulfilling of our comforts and desires. This proves true when someone challenges the idea of God's love towards us concerning sin. We hear about the sacrifice of Jesus Christ and enjoy speaking of the love God showed in this while we were sinning. Then we dismiss the necessity of living righteous lives in respect of that sacrifice. I have heard many excuse their sinful ways with a blanket statement of God loves me regardless. I remember making the same statement during my deception. As if the issue at hand is God's love when we act ignorant of doing what we know is right. I hope this statement lands home for all who will ever read this. Everything that has ever happened in the world on a grand and minor scale in each individual life ever lived, has **NEVER** been about the lack of love God had for anyone. **It has always been about our lack of love towards him.** Now that's very challenging for many to receive yet no one can stand before God and say they lived every second of their life in obedience to him. So, when our soul stands before him in judgement, it will not be about how much God didn't love a person. No, the blood of Jesus has already proven his love. It will be about how we either lived our lives in respect of that sacrifice or in rejection of it.

Selfish love is hypocrisy

Although thought comes prior to faith, faith illuminates the thought because thought requires faith to have power. Therefore, the mind needs discipline and self-control. For it can be manipulated and its ways can deceive itself. For if I only apply my **experiences** or my **learned ideas** to a matter such as what love is, then what I present to people can only be my idea of what I've known. Whenever anything is presented as a form of self it has a root of selfishness. For example, if I love to serve in the church because it makes me feel good. Makes me feel needed. Then my form of serving has nothing to do with others. I am serving with a form of self. This deception from within is hard to see as a lie for it disregards the right heart. **This idea of love is a form of what I get in return**. Usually, you will find very discontent individuals serving in the church because of this very reality. You see, this is a form of love many believe is right although it is not true love according to the gospel, we say we believe in. **Love is not self-serving or self-seeking**. This is how people try to manipulate God as if it were possible. Doing what presents itself as love but not seeking the love of God in their heart's prior. This is clearly important to God and something he truly desires us to understand. His son literally informed us to leave your offering at the alter and first go and reconcile the discourse that exists in you with a brother first. God is not blinded by our service to him to where he dismisses the condition of the heart. It is written that God sees obedience better than sacrifice. Be not confused, Jesus was obedient prior to giving himself as a sacrifice. I would even go as far to say no one is able to truly sacrifice anything from a pure heart without a life of obedience first. This means God wants our lives to live in him more than our moments of service to him. That is a very challenging word that requires a spiritual understanding. If this is challenging to receive, please pray and ask for clarity from the Holy Spirit. Along with all things you read in this book please study to show this approved in scripture.

Our desires create a false Jesus

A question that seems to circulate amongst the world and believers is about God loving sinners. Both are asking a truly pointless question that is wrapped in ignorance, because he has already shown his love towards us **while** we were in sin. What love have we shown him in response to that, is the question. **The love of God will not excuse a sinner whom either rejected the sacrifice of Jesus Christ or claimed to receive it but lived without respect to it.** When many desire to reject this, it shows the lack of knowing him. When we don't know him, we characterize him as whatever fits our desires. With that, you see this true when people speak statements like these. **"We will always sin"** or **"God knows my heart" "Love is Love"** or **"Jesus would have supported the LGBTQ"** or **"God make me a millionaire"** or **"God change my spouse" "God help me get this car or job or business etc.."** or the famous **"God what is my purpose"**. All these sorts of assumptions, questions and requests dominate the understanding of the world claiming to know Christ. Those sayings are based on emotions and desires of the world. Yet it is common to speak this way towards God. Mainly because many don't know him! This basis of God's love is supported by what we can get from him, or how he can agree with our desires. Ironically the most important thing we got from him we rarely speak of daily when referencing him. The very salvation and saving grace he bestowed upon us is the very conversation many get tired of having or hearing. They want more. God has more for your life it is said. What is the more? If it is outside of living righteously and Holy as a response to the very grace and mercy upon our lives, then we are sadly mistaken and are deceived in thinking we know God. For we know inside that God is love. The world and our experiences look to shape that understanding into its own for us. Here is the point. All of us learned the idea of love from emotional interactions. We also learned respect from seeking those we have things in common with. Therefore, our view of God is broken, and yet there is a false love faith-belief that claims to know God because we know love and respect from those ways. Until we abandon the idea we know God, we will never desire to truly know him the way He intended us to know him. Not the love we have learned or the love we believe we have within ourselves. Rather his love through Christ Jesus. That love corrects and rebukes. In classic Satanic form many attempt to reject this with scripture, by calling correction, condemnation. Condemnation is real when we leave this body if we used this body to live a life against God. While were in this flesh it be better to turn from the ways that will condemn us rather than live deceived, attempting to manipulate the patience of God. For in the end, it is not God that will condemn us but our very ways of living that will stand as our condemnation. For it is written in **John 3:19** that the world has already been judged, and this is the judgement, that the light came into the world and man loved his darkness more, because their **deeds were evil.**

There are many tricks of the devil to keep a person from taking responsibility for their actions. Many tricks of the devil that have many rebuking the Holy Spirit when it comes and speaks a word to them to change their ways. Many times, the corrective word or discipline from God is rebuked because of hardship. What sorrow will come when many that claimed to know God find that they lived their lives rebuking the very Holy Spirit that was sent to reveal all truth to them. It's because again we never learned the love of God or respected his love as one that does this for those he loves.

Revelations 3:19 Those whom I love, I rebuke and discipline, therefore be zealous and repent.

A world ignorant of love

The world cannot define what love is without God. For he is love. No-one would ever ask a newborn to write a paper on the trials of adulthood. For one, we understand the obvious. The newborn cannot write, nor formulate a thought completely for another to understand the topic nor understand it for themselves. I hope all get this. Asking the world about love is like asking an infant to articulate clearly to you anything, let alone on a topic they have no experience in. Just as the infant must learn to communicate effectively from one who is able, the world must learn love from God who is love. **Seek the one that is the topic.** God introduced the proper way to love through his son. The one that came in the name of love, you would think his views would be valuable. Yet he was rejected. His ways, his history, his works. Rejected. For the light came into the world and man loved their darkness more. This is the judgement God has finalized for the world. There is nothing more just than this from God.

This generation brings this parable to mind. There were parents that decided to listen to their 6-year-old tell them how to budget their bank account and pay the bills. They did not want to correct the child as the child was able to articulate words that were above the knowledge level they expected. So, they decided to give their 6-year-old access to the bank accounts and all the funds. They allowed them to pay the bills and made them responsible to remember when they were due. The parents decide not to check on how the child is doing because they feel the child made good points when speaking to them on how it should be done. Once the parents did this, they decided to go public and share with the world their decision, and many other parents decided to do the same with their children. It became a trend, and the entire world began to follow this with their children. Immediately many started finding themselves in hardships and in financial crisis. Instead of all the parents addressing their lack of wisdom used to get in this position, they all formed a plan to hide the disfunction and maintain the lie that it is working for them. Because of this a generation of children grew up with stress and frustrations from having such responsibilities on their shoulders. Even the stress and frustrations of the children were hidden by the parents to keep the lie in place. All done in fear that their lack of wisdom would be exposed. This is the world. What a vain and corrupt generation! Not one parent would do this, yet you see many giving great responsibilities to children. Just not financial ones for then parents would be directly harmed, so they allow the children to make decisions that will only affect themselves negatively.

This is the world's idea of love. God makes it clear how we should live and there is wisdom found in his ways completely. Instead of doing things the way God instructs, mankind elects to create a new way. A way without basic common sense or any regard for success within it to flourish, but because it is their own way, they fight to keep it and maintain it. Even to the degree of hiding the failures and flaws within their way. So far to the point that using children as pawns to push the darkness in their hearts is seen as necessary. God is just in his verdict against this world. It ignores its hardships and masks it's sadness just to maintain the unwise ways it has chosen against God that has loved them. May the Holy Spirit discern this parable for all who desire to understand.

A false inward nature

What manner of faith can exist amongst falsehoods? The desire to claim faith in what is Holy and pure is impossible with an unclean heart. This is the presentation of love now that conflicts within us. It's the desire to receive our own view of love from our experiences that drives the emotion to reject true love. Yes, it's psychological for everything is and will be. For your mind is individually your own. No-one has another's yet we all have had the mind of sin. We all need to learn true love, but none of us needed to learn sin. This means our very nature of being was lost. We see this in many ways like so. Manipulation, jealousy, envy, lying, and greed. This all is displayed within our false nature. All stemming from the desire to get what we want. We even see this in areas of intimate relationships. People can be very good at playing roles to maintain relationships for selfish reasons. Hiding their true feelings on matters of the heart. Calling this love while inside raging against the person they are joined with. You see this happens a lot of times in marriages. The idea that if we keep the marriage intact for the sake of the children they will benefit. Disregarding the very interaction of the marriage, as essential. You see, even in man's attempt to do right it shows as corrupt without God. Sadly, many tell their spouses "I love you daily for years to keep this false inward nature that produces a false outward nature. Never able to truly grasp the concept that marriage is about your spouse not yourself. Serving another and being submitted to God in Christ to love selflessly is marriage. So instead of trying to support what is false, the requirement is to learn what is true and live it outwardly. This is the invisible reality we all understand. Our thoughts. Our contemplations. This is who we truly are. So, it should make sense that those hidden, and secretive invisibilities are 100% what each person has faith in. This isn't about words, or even actions. No this is about the unheard, unseen, reality we all can agree on that exists in us all. The thought. When it becomes nurtured on God in his word and matures within us, it will evolve into the correct display of love towards others. This is what the scripture means in **Galatians 6:7-8** when it says be not deceived, whatsoever a man soweth, that shall he reap. The man that sows to please his flesh, from the flesh shall reap destruction, but the one who sows to please the Spirit, from the Spirit shall reap eternal life.

We all at some point took from experiences that have influenced us to formulate our thoughts. Thinking about it is our own independent idea. With that said, faith is not a foreign word or idea. For it is the basis of all we know. For nothing within us begins without it.

There is a wide array of possibilities to present our unique thought "we claim" and relay it to others. If these thoughts are from Satan, we are used by him so that thought can reside within us. Therefore, the scripture tells us to resist Satan and he will flee. This is speaking to how you deal with thoughts that are not from God's word. We place faith in the thought for it to have power. This power from faith, whether through sound or action, creates its existence. So, you see we use faith every day. Our very inward nature is a production of faith. If we never had faith in our thoughts, our actions and our words would never exist. We are either living from a place of faith in Jesus or Satan. The very outward nature of ourselves is the display of our faith in whatever we believe in. Whatever we have trusted as true within our frame of thinking that is. Having said all that, I can only conclude that the love that one presents to another is the form of love that one has placed their faith in. The false love faith from Satan or the true inward nature of Christ. In that very nature of faith, we have the free will to receive the teachings and ways of God through his son Jesus. Thereby proving our thoughts on what true love is and our outward nature will reflect what is within. It is written and was taught by the Christ to clean the inside of the cup and the outside will be clean also. This means that our very idea of love that we have placed faith in shall always be the display we present to others. Also, it means that once we truly accept the right view from God on love through Christ, we can present it in its proper form. For what we **believe** love is can **never** replace **who** love is. We can only know true love through believing in him.

True submission disarms lies

Comfort, peace, joy, self-control, truth, and life without death spiritually has been given to all of us that have faith in Jesus Christ. No-one can prevent you from receiving this through Christ, but your idea of love can. Don't let anyone attempt to do anything against the truth. We should only present the truth in its just form from Christ. **It needs no formal presentation through entertainment or boasting of itself.** For that is not found within it. If there is anyone that forgets, let him remember. Everyone that hates correction hates God's love. No one can receive him while proud. No-one can receive him believing they are not what he says they are. The entire faith begins with repentance. How can anyone claim to love Jesus while clinging to the idea that they are not truly a sinful person that has lived against God in all their ways? Why would such a person even contemplate needing a savior? It is clearly the reason for the animosity against God. God is informing everyone that you are not as great as you think you are. In fact, you are wretched and wicked, promised to perish from the ways of living displayed. The arrogant cannot handle such a message, let alone the message that informs them that to make this relationship right there must be a complete submission to him. There must be a complete belief in the fact that what he says is true and not what the world says. Not what my family and friends say, or what my favorite celebrity says in an interview. What God says only. That is what prevents mankind from coming to God with all their hearts. They value and love their own form of love which is darkness. Do not value all those in the world and all their personal desires and opinions more than Christ. He is correcting them, and they do not want correction. They want to display their faith in their own beliefs. How bold they are and confident in their error.

The most disappointing aspect of this is how so many professing Christians cower under fear and adapt their way of thinking to the world in hopes of keeping comfort on earth.

Everyone that submits to this world and agrees with it or simply goes along with what it does is received by the world. All that speak out against obvious and blatant attempts to spread darkness are considered the problem. Well according to their desires and plans, we are their problem, but we prefer to present the solution. We are carriers of the light, and we know who has the power to give them life and life eternally. They confuse us to be naive believers, yet we are living breathing proof that a person can be changed by the power of God. The light from God in us is what stirs the world to anger. Here we are as foreigners awaiting our Lord and we exist where evil desires to dominate. We won't go silently, and the world desires us to do so because the more the light shines here it exposes the darkness. We constantly confound the world by loving the person and abhorring sin. The world is training many to believe there is no possible separation of oneself from the sin that is a lifestyle. The gospel disarms this lie. For there is but darkness here and the last thing evil wants is for anyone to see the light. For if the light is seen then it reveals the lie and disarms it for the one who believes in the truth. This is clearly why you hear statements like "what is truth" or "live your truth". Darkness cannot do anything against the truth. It simply wants to create its own.

In the day the Lord provides remember the truth in Christ. Let the invisible but visible, the powerful but merciful, the unique but simple, God in Christ Jesus be shown to the world. Christ must be given to so that the darkness can be revealed. I tell you the truth, not one single person can discern the darkness in this world without light. Jesus is the light of God. **Read John 8:12**. He was the food and the water for us all that wish to consume Him. His very body and his blood. The true inward nature in his body carried outwardly is our example. The shedding of his blood through the sacrifice of his life, is our atonement for sin. Yes, correction is needed just as a disrespectful child requires a firm parent. We all needed this, for we were disrespectful in every way towards God. As it is written, WHILE we were yet sinners God showed his love to us by sending his son. True belief in that, submits to it gladly and finds peace. Peace comes once the lie is disarmed. This is why Jesus states that IF you continue in his word, you are truly his disciples, then you will know the truth and the truth will make you free.

Worship in Spirit and in truth

Everything evil in this world is celebrated by the world.

From the confusion to the nonsense. From lust and

pride to anger and selfishness. All are celebrated.

Knowledge of life through Christ is real and everything

else is creative darkness from forgetfulness. We

celebrate Christ and life in him. For it is not of this

world though we be in it temporarily. God will never

tell you to love something he has condemned. Again,

there is no lifestyle God has condemned as sin that

he now approves of and wants his followers to love.

Love the person, not the sinful lifestyle. The false love

faith movement has convinced people living in their

147

lifestyles against God that all should love their way of life. Yet these things cannot produce life. So, they are asking you to love death. We cannot love death for we have already died and are now alive in Christ. No-one can put such shackles back on us. To see the self-professing Christian place such shackles back on themselves for the admiration of those that delight themselves in death, brings a sorrow we shouldn't have to experience. God forbid our minds stay in such a thought long enough to picture such a fate for them. Let our faith stand on what is already done and let us be more confident in that just as those that do not desire Christ (the truth) are confident in themselves. We await our Lord with hope and confidence that he is for us. It is beyond time fellow believers put away their petty ideological differences and stand as one in Christ. It is beyond time we as believers put away the pride and arrogance to be separate from each other for denomination's sake and stand on the faith in Jesus Christ. Let all of us clearly see the times we are living in and live with urgency for the time that has been at hand. **God forbid this is read with contempt.**

Is there any surprise that seeking all of God is much more challenging than presenting ourselves as good by doing good things? God requires the heart to be right first. This is a difficult word for many to receive as they have agreed with their truth for so long and have faith in it. Their truth is, if a person is doing good things, God must be in their heart, right? The answer is maybe. The realization that God prefers your motives over your deeds is hard to accept by those that wish to simply portray their version of love rather than seek his. You see, love doesn't have many forms. Pride and selfishness desire many forms for they despise how they truly look. So often they will use the appearance of love to carry out their true intent. That intent is to serve themselves. Unfortunately, a person's version of love is what's used as a blanket to cover those true emotions. Make no mistake there is an enemy of God in this world. We must examine that enemy within us first. Place your faith with the truth in Christ. For there is only one truth. It is Satan that has transformed himself into an angel of light. This means he is using the cover of good to carry out his evil. Without Christ this mask to the world is sufficient and they cannot tell the difference for their hearts are dark and lost. He is mimicking the deeds, the words, the service of the church to appear as one with the same heart. He is easily seen if you are in Christ. If you are not truly in Christ, Satan knows how to act and speak to present himself as pure hearted. For our Lord informed us to beware of wolves in sheep clothing.

Notice he didn't say, beware of wolves. It is not the wolf you can clearly see that you should beware of. He ensured we understood that the one you should beware of will not present himself as a wolf. He then informs us that we will know them by their fruit. We mistake fruit for deeds. **Make no mistake, your fruit is not the deeds you do**. Your fruit is the very character you display from the Holy Spirit to all. In all circumstances and challenges. That character from God does produce good deeds but **the evil one simply desires deeds to mask the character**. So, examine yourselves, examine your motives! God forbid any of us come to find that we were actually wolves masking as sheep to others. I can only give God the glory that he spared this once deceived wolf that thought he was a sheep. Because of this, I am now like Paul, a true bond servant of the Lord. For our sins were great, to the degree we consider ourselves once chiefs of sin. This be my effort in these last days to alarm all that claim Christ to examine themselves deeply from within and desire a pure heart.

True character is shown in trials

It is written by Paul the apostle that we are to delight ourselves in tribulation. That's a jaw dropping statement. Especially with a hoard of believers that have been taught to pray for yourself that you may be brought out of tribulations. What has become lost in this desire to not go through what Jesus said we would, is the fact that God allows this. He allows the trials and difficulties. It's like we think Satan has some authority over God here on earth. Everything taking place is being allowed by God, because he does not see Satan as a threat to him. We see Satan as a threat and give him more regard than the Holy Spirit.

There is fear when Satan is spoken of by many, and this shows a lack of knowledge towards Christ Jesus. Did we not read that when demons saw Jesus approaching, they begged for mercy that he would not torture them. I honestly believe that many are living without the true fear of God. Rather a fear of Satan and this is why evil knows how to break our character. If we cling to this life and the pleasures of the world, the evil one knows to simply attack that area. Then our character, our faith, and our integrity in Christ will crumble. Praise God that Shadrach, Meshach, and Abednego understood the truth. For as it is written, the fire did not touch them, nor did they even smell of smoke. It is not fire or the persecution that was the issue. For that was nothing to God for he allowed it. Rather it is our faith in him during it that he is observing. It is our understanding during it that is exposed as well as our character. **This lets us know**

without doubt that the evil one wants us to pay attention to the circumstances he presents and desires our faith in it. The only way any of us will be able to delight ourselves in tribulation is with the right vision of God's love. That produces true faith in him as we endure it. During this time the only way we can spot the evil one from within us is how we live the truth in Christ. It's the only way we can examine ourselves to know if we are trusting in the only truth. For no one can say their truth is that they will stand firm in God without a trial or tribulation. Examine how you are dealing with trials in your current life. How do you truly think towards them? How do you truly pray for them? This is a microcosm of how you would seriously handle persecution for your faith. Do not be deceived, if you are stressed out and emotionally all over the place because of the trials of life, this is God allowing you to see who you truly are currently. Think not that you would stand firm in Christ if your actual life was threatened or jailed. Do not live with a belief that you can suddenly flip a switch and alter your character for the sake of Christ if not doing so prior to persecution. You either have the Holy Spirits character in your everyday life or you don't. If you have the character of the Holy Spirit in you, then once the trial or tribulation shows up concerning the faith, you are simply applying who you already are in him. This is the truth, do not be deceived. Take the account and the words from the one who has seen this true in myself and others. Start this very day applying faith towards the challenges in your life. Everything you are experiencing has a purpose towards molding your character into righteousness. As it is written in Romans 5:3-5 We rejoice in our sufferings, knowing our sufferings produces endurance, and endurance produces character and character produces hope. Hope does not put us to shame because God in his love has poured out into our hearts through his Holy Spirit whom he gave to us. When we truly want a pure inward nature towards God, then we can read this verse and understand it completely. Not only that but can believe it with our lives. Have faith in that love, for yes, it is true.

(chamishi) חֲ מִ ישׁ י

<u>Victorious Truth</u>

Yeshua, which is the Hebrew name for Jesus, said
that if you stay in his word, you will know the truth and
it will make you free. **Free!** This world and its self-
created chaos have done a great job of trying to
display to us what freedom is and isn't. A very
unfortunate example of this being played out as we
speak is what has plagued the community of African
Americans. Due to a past in this country concerning

slavery and mistreatment. The very idea presented is that your freedom is based on the physical circumstances you experience alone. This is the very bait Satan has used to give many the haughty eyes of worldly advancement in this community. It is the very bait Satan has used to bound many in this community and others mentally. I am very aware that this topic is one that many stay away from considering the guaranteed backlash it will bring. What is more important than any backlash from this community is the truth. I grew up in this community and my heritage aligns with it so for those who think themselves equipped to speak on this, I guess I qualify. Amongst my fellow African Americans, I have seen casual negative racial notions towards their very own race. Much of which I will not mention here as to even speak of what evil does in secret is disgraceful. What I will say is this. **There is no truth existing in the**

mindset that looks to the past for fuel to motivate today's anger. Oh, how so many have departed from the faith because of the actions of others. So many looking to the past to justify their current strife, to justify their outrage. Looking to the lives of others to guide their understanding concerning freedom. What often gets lost amongst a generation that screams about the wrongs of slavery is how they disregard that generation that was united in morals and humility. If anyone from that generation of slavery were able to see what some of their future descendants currently act like, they would be disgusted and confused. Many of them had strong faith in Christ amongst cruelties they experienced. Many of them didn't even receive the word of God in completion or in truth, yet even while their faith was tested it remained strong for some. Many of them were not allowed to read or write let alone have a bible for themselves. What excuse do we have to not conduct ourselves according to the word of God?! Unfortunately, a spoiled and confused generation would come many years later tugging at the hymn of their shirts as a scapegoat to act out. What an absolute travesty to live amongst such a disrespectful generation. I hope this frees someone; I truly hope someone abandons the lie that uses hardships of others to justify their nonsense. You are not for them; you are against them when you act in ways they would have never agreed with. As for those that believe they can point to the past and blame those in the current for what their ancestors did, I would like to expose something major here.

Hypocrisy enslaves

The last thing anyone of us should want God to do is hold us accountable for the actions of our ancestors. I have heard many speak in the most demeaning ways towards their very own parents. Many reference the very lives their parents have lived with an iron judgement towards them. This exists amongst all ethnicities. Every child somehow has the best judgement when it comes to their parents. So many children do not desire to even answer for the actions of their parents as that would be so unfair to them. Yet there is a sect of African Americans that believe their ancestors are the true Hebrews that were enslaved in Egypt, the true Jews that were led into Israel. While this sect of so-called believers announces what they believe is biblical consequences against one heritage they excuse their own. They surely do not claim that they must answer for the sins of their own so-called ancestors. They quote the prophets and then skip over every account given from those very same prophets on how the children of

Israel rebelled against God constantly. My question to them is simply this. If God does not hold you accountable for the sins of your ancestors, then how can we want any European or so-called Gentile to answer for theirs. What manner of hypocrisy is this? Have we not read that God's chosen people rebelled against him several times and suffered many consequences in doing so. Are we not to answer for what they did? The best way to address those that ignore biblical truths will be the same way Jesus addressed the Sadducees in **Matthew 22:29**. These men presented Jesus with a hypothetical scenario about marriage in the afterlife. Thinking themselves clever they exposed their own ignorance. Jesus tells them **you are mistaken because you do not know the scriptures or the power of God**. Anyone trying to block someone from receiving the saving grace of God through his son Jesus because of their heritage needs to understand what Jesus is saying here. If the covenant of marriage is null and void in the resurrection, why would your heritage in the flesh be considered? No human has ever made a covenant with their heritage prior to being born. Not even one. A covenant must be chosen, it must have the consent of two to be entered when concerning two people. Not one of us had a say in what heritage we would be born into, so how could we make a covenant with it. The Hebrews did not do anything to cause God to choose them. God did this according to his perfect plan and that covenant he made with Abraham he sealed with himself. The covenant he made with Abraham never excused the actions of his descendants when they came. They still received punishments even to the degree that God voiced a desire to end them as they rebelled in the wilderness. The answer that aligns with the word of God is that your heritage is not considered and thank God it isn't. Could you imagine living your life following Christ as your Lord, and when that life ends you stand before him and hear him say well done good and faithful servant, but also, I have this one thing against you. Your heritage rebelled against me and carried out evil ways. You must answer for them just as they must answer for themselves. What Bible is being read that believes Jesus will address anyone in this manner? There isn't one true to the gospel that informs us of this. In fact, we have clearly documented scripture in Revelations 7:9 that tells us there will be a multitude too large to count from every nation and tribe and people and tongue. This multitude will be standing before the throne and the lamb, clothed in white with palm branches in hand speaking something very clearly as worship. They will say "Salvation to our God who sits on the throne and to the Lamb!" With this you see very clearly heaven will have no regard for heritage as all who believed will be present.

We also have scripture from the prophet Jeremiah where in chapter 31:27-34 a new covenant is declared from the Lord. This new covenant specifically says that God will sow into the house of Israel and the house of Judah the seed of man and of beast. Now this may sound confusing but really all you must do is ask yourself this. If the house of Israel and the house of Judah are God's chosen people that he led out of bondage in Egypt. Who must be the seed of man and of beast he planned to sow into them? Well, who is left? Obviously, those without the heritage of the house of Israel and the house of Judah. To add to this evidence, we have the prophet Isaiah speaking the word from God concerning Gentiles coming to the Lord in chapter 56:1-8. We also find evidence in John 10:16 where Jesus states there are other sheep that are not of this fold, I must bring them in as well, they will listen to my voice. Then there will be one flock and one shepherd. This all shows there is no biblical support for the idea that only those with African or Hispanic heritage can be saved. Let alone their heritage being a factor concerning God's salvation. Anyone that has a problem with this information has a problem with God. For it is God that spoke this to his prophets, and it is he that sent his son Yeshua to give his life for it, thereby fulfilling it.

True freedom is peace in Christ

I used to wonder how Paul understood his freedom in Christ while in prison. How did Stephen understand his freedom while being stoned? Did John perceive his freedom while being boiled in oil? Not only did they understand their freedom, but they were victorious in the truth. That victorious truth is that this flesh cannot dictate my freedom. Nothing done to it while we live in it can take my freedom. While the mind is consumed by the attraction of the world it is impossible for anyone to receive this. Amongst my community of African Americans there has been a strong shift towards abandoning the faith for beliefs in cultural practices found in Africa. This deceiving desire to connect with one's culture has presented a sense of freedom to many. While this false sense of freedom is received, pagan and mystical practices are welcomed. While my sorrow is immense concerning this, I simply receive what the Holy Spirit has informed me. Those that leave the faith for this do not understand what family they belonged to. They sought after the family of the flesh and rejected the family of the spirit. Therefore, they are not my siblings but those who place their faith in the Lord Jesus Christ are. For it is written that there is no longer Jew or Gentile, but all are one in the faith. I don't care how many false pictures of Christ exist, that does not have the power to alter his words. I don't care how many professing Christians exist that have lived hypocritically to what the gospel says. That does not have the power to change the truth in God. So much of what people have against the word of God is based on what they have seen from people that claim the faith. We do not remotely treat anything with the same contempt. In fact, many will be silent towards their close relatives concerning behaviors and habits that they know will bring demise. I cannot speak of any other culture or race of people but mine. This is the norm and is celebrated amongst them. Out of the same mouth that yells black lives matter, is the same mouth that raps about killing that life. Out of the same mouth that professes the importance of the black family comes the hypocrisy to support the LGBTQ community. A community that supports abortion yet cannot produce a child through its lifestyle but will adopt one. I could go one but as I type these very things my heart becomes heavy. My desire is that all regardless their cultural background may come to the truth in Christ. My hope for them is that the lie and the hypocrisy of culture be disabled. The desire to find purpose and identity can only be fulfilled in Christ. My sincere hope for them is this truth. Without it the curse stays intact and the very rebellious ways of our ancestors the prophets depicted stays.

The curse of hypocrisy

There is no victory in cultural beliefs that produces darkness. Just hypocrisy and the desire to ignore hypocrisy as if irrelevant. This entire agenda is to keep one's mind on the flesh. It uses emotional manipulation and preys on the past to invoke ignorance to the present. This generation has not even seen the hardships of those that once fought for basic citizen rights here in this country. With that said, I will do my best to help shine a light so the deception that is running rampant in this community and others like it can be exposed. So here is what the Holy Spirit has placed upon my heart concerning this. This is what the evil one is doing. He is looking to keep your minds on the flesh. He cannot speak to spiritual freedom because he cannot provide it. His basis is the flesh and all it has created. He will claim to present freedom from physical bondage by manners of materialism and your worldly advancement. Again, this freedom the world presents is only through things of the world.

Notice when slavery is brought up, we never hear who truly was the first to free slaves. In this country, the account of Moses and Aaron being sent by God to free the Hebrews from Egypt is rarely told as the first freeing of slaves from physical bondage. Rather everyone references Abraham Lincoln or the civil rights movement. Notice how the very people that claim to be strong and independent in thought still align their history with those they claim are wrong. **Those that enslaved others are now rejected for those ways. Yet the mentality of a lot of those individuals that dishonored their slaves, now shows present in the race that was enslaved.** What could I possibly mean by this? If you have read the teachings of Jesus Christ, you see clearly what I mean. If you are angry what makes you different from another angry person? If you hate someone because of their skin what makes you different from the one that hates you, because of yours? This shows a blindness of hypocrisy, and it only comes by way of envy and pride. I have found that many in my community don't disagree with racism. They just don't like it when it's directed at them. There is a vengeful and hateful spirit that is breeding the idea of it's our turn to carry out what was done to us in this community. Those who exist with that Spirit always find themselves rejecting responsibility for their choices. There is no desire to seek Christ, so they turn to worldly ways, wishing to use the hardships of previous generations to excuse poor choices while utilizing anger. Is this not true? If this is contested by anyone, then what manner of oppression causes us to have no free will? Just because your circumstances are challenging doesn't mean your free will is removed. Did Shadrach, Meshach and Abednego have free will while they were being threatened with fire? Of course, they did. They used their free will to honor God regardless the hardship. This generation desires everyone to excuse their free will because of hardships. Most of which are not true hardships but rather consequences from poor choices. This will raise some eyebrows, but it is the truth. My loyalty is to the God of Abraham, Issac and Jacob in Christ Jesus. That loyalty will require me to always speak the truth. Come out of this bondage my people and see you are what you claim to hate!

Chosen mental slavery

Be not deceived, even God leading the people to Israel didn't free their mentalities. They were angry with God, complained, and even wished that they return to their physical bondage. This is important to understand. Physical freedom does not assure mental or spiritual freedom. For if your only concern is physical freedom, then you are satisfied with the things of this world alone. A career, money, recognition, a home, a vehicle. All placed to satisfy your flesh. We never view them as the bondage that enslaves us to this world, mainly because we are told we **own** these things. Unfortunately, many want possessions for themselves, not to sustain life for their family and generations after. We are told that reaching these things will supply a good life. We have been groomed to accept this and yet once we accept it **our lust for these things removes our understanding of God.** For the <u>love</u> of money is the root of all evil. There have been many despicable and wicked things done for the simple desire to increase and advance in this world. **This is slavery above all else.** That is the slavery that the evil one wants you to be under. This has nothing to do with race or religion.

The evil one desires this bondage for all, while God desires all to be free from it.

Many ideas have been indoctrinated into our social and spiritual worlds. Ideas that have many praying for worldly things as a requirement. Thoughts and questions begin to surface and the very faith in Christ is more of an afterthought. Ultimately truth is under attack when we think or speak about our desires for the world. This gives birth to stress, anxiety, and frustration towards God. **Be not deceived, if your mind is upon the things of the world, then it is enslaved to the world and its worldly desires**. Is life not more than what you eat or wear? This question was asked by our Savior. It is very challenging to hear him when you have preachers and those that claim Christ all giving another message. That message is these things should be your focus. The follow up to that message is always, God desires to bless you with these things. Christ told us to seek the kingdom of God and all his righteousness, and he would add these things to you. We hear teachings like work hard at getting these things and bring Christ along with you. It's a message teaching the truth in reverse. This is why it is so hard to spot it unless the preacher becomes so full of himself that his complete preaching and focus is directed towards materialistic prosperity. Don't think for a second that the person consumed by career aspirations or desiring their so-called purpose in the world is praying for those things because they love God. No these are prayers in rejection of God. At best they are doing this deceived and truly believe he is for their worldly desires. This is unfortunate for this is the best-case scenario! At worst they despise God and are willfully trying to manipulate others for gain while using the son of God as a cover. This mental slavery is so often chosen with delight. It is slavery that presents itself as freedom. Freedom to want a more comfortable and fulfilling worldly life. Not a spiritual one in Christ. We must study the word of God and renew our minds in it to know truth. Then the Holy Spirit will reveal all truth to us. This will grant discernment; this is not talked about enough as being a necessary aspect in our walk. There are clever teachings that attempt to appeal to what is already desired by this flesh. They are impossible to recognize without discernment. Here is proof. Jesus says this, is not life more than what you eat or what you wear? This is a commonly known word spoken by Jesus yet many claim him and their focus is what they will eat and what they will wear. How is it possible to do the opposite of who you claim to follow? This shows the weakness of our flesh. We all see that the sow a seed teaching is only intended to focus on money. Yet if we love money, the teaching is received. Don't we see the speak it into existence ministry only concerns itself with materialistic worldly items and gain? We see it but we love materialistic things and the euphoric feeling of gain in this world. The teachings of Christ have been provided; the sacrifice has been given. Freedom is in place for all that choose to not enslave themselves to their flesh desires in the world. When our desire becomes truly Christ, his teachings are deeply welcomed, and the desires of the world begin to perish. Now consider this, when our desires are in the world, the love for Christ begins to perish within us. This is why it is written, if anyone loves the world, the love of the father is not in them. I am telling the truth in Christ, I am not lying, my conscience testifies with me in the Holy Spirit. Sow into the spirit and you will reap eternal life. Ask God for the fruits of the Spirit to be present in you over every interaction, and a heart from God will bear much fruit. The flesh could care less about this, while the spirit craves for us to have this deeply. This will free the mind and focus it on freedom not bondage.

The sorrow of truth

It brings great sorrow to tell you that you will have trials in this world. Even if avoiding the world, it will come to meet you. This world hates Christ. It hates the truth. Nonetheless you have been separated. Separated to receive the truth without arrogance or pride. Rather receive this truth spiritually to live. This world is beneath God and its ways are not of God, not even its thoughts. Now find yourself not a burden to anyone lest your shame be full. For if you do burden someone and feel no shame, then your pride is full of selfishness, and your selfishness is full of error and foolishness. Seek the way to love purely as it is written to do so. Why be married to error? Error is so blatant during these times that even some non-believers can see it for what it is. The deep sorrow of this truth is that some self-proclaiming Christians can't seem to see it for what it is. How that is possible is beyond me. What I will say is this. The first to be cast into the lake of fire in **Revelations 21:8** are **cowards**. Yes cowards, meaning this must be the Christians that heard the truth, but didn't share it out of fear of persecution or even just not being liked by the world. So, it's not that some of these self-professing believers cannot see the error, they willfully turn a blind eye to it. How deeply cruel it is to disregard the unwavering consequences someone will endure from their ways, just to keep your personal comfort here on earth. The sorrow of truth is that someone may not like you for sharing it. Yet true love is willing to be rejected by a loved one, stranger or family member in hopes they might be saved. On the other hand, you will hear this world claim various forms of truth. Ideas like a person shouldn't reject what we know as sinful ways within themselves. An idea such as, it isn't a sin if they simply feel it is who they are. Even going as far to say they should claim it as an identity. Not stopping there, they desire that person to boast in it and parade around in it with arrogance and pride. What a deep pit the devil has dug for people seeking purpose and identity from the world. Once again you see it is always based on the flesh. Everything the evil one desires to keep us in bondage to resides within the flesh. He has used every single aspect of the flesh to carry out this. From the color of the flesh to the thoughts of the flesh to the desires of the flesh. We are living amongst the generation that celebrates the flesh. This can be so hard to see but it is a direct mockery of God. A generation that rages out against the punishments from God. The consequences from their decisions. Then arrogantly ask questions like where's God when things take place they do not understand. The key to understanding the gospel of Jesus Christ is to know the truth must be applied across the board to everyone. If it is not, then it cannot be the truth. The world wishes to only apply its ideals, it's morals to those who align with its agenda to rebel against God. Everyone that does not conform is the problem and since the ascension of Jesus Christ every true believer has faced ridicule, rejection, and persecution from this world. This will not stop until the return of our Lord, so make the choice today whom you desire to stand with.

God shall not be mocked

Make no mistake, God is not mocked. Whatever is sown shall be reaped. So, the same people that are called criminals now, will eventually have a ground of defense to stand on for their behaviors. This is due to the senseless lies that have been pushed on a generation to receive sinful behavior as love. Claiming for the betterment of peace, and this has ultimately given birth to a new idea of what family can look like. What attraction is acceptable and what form of thinking should be received by society as norms. There will be no recovery from this blasphemous change the world has received as good. So, it shall reap all it has sown. Remember this. True spiritual life in Christ is much greater than a person's environment or family or upbringing. **You must be born again**. Your mind must be baptized with the fire of Jesus Christ. Meaning you must choose to think as he did. Follow his understanding and not only will you be above this world mentally but nothing in it will have the power to imprison your mind. With that said think not highly of yourself. For it is only by the grace of God you will be able to do anything according to his wonderful will. You of yourself can do nothing. This flesh you have withers just like everyone else's. You are to be a servant of the Lord. If you choose not to be, don't forget God is not mocked. You will serve someone or something here on earth even if it is yourself. A just and righteous God allows everyone to reap what they have sown into during their life. To the one that sows into sexual perversion, disease and consequences of lust are reaped. To the one that sows into lies, hypocrisy and confusion is reaped. To the one that sows into anger, uncontrollable outburst and shame is reaped. You will find the same reaping from all ways against God. As for those who sow into the spirit with belief in Jesus Christ. Life everlasting is reaped, and a harvest of delicious fruit that produces righteousness!!

True Purpose Revealed

The word purpose is a very popular word. One that captivates all of mankind. It has been manipulated by Satan to confuse many. Now as a Christian it has been said that **our purpose** needs to be found. Many skills or talents can reveal **your** purpose it is said. Let's see what the word of God says about **our** purpose. The subtleness of the evil one always can be found within the little details of trying to appeal to your desires for self and not God. We are here to bring glory to the Highest Father and his kingdom. The importance of this cannot be overstated. Many miss this due to the flesh's desire to fulfill its purpose. To feel like you are accomplishing something here to further your name. Be on guard against this as it is a trick of the devil. It is written that we are here to suffer for Christ. So, any trial or tribulation that comes your way is not to be feared or worried about. It is to be expected and you are to understand that the comfort of life has destroyed many. Again, I say read. Renew your mind daily. This will help you re-focus on Christ and not yourself. This topic can be very challenging because our gifts and talents God has given can all be used to help our brothers and sisters. The deceiver is aware of this so he will try and get you to use those talents and gifts to serve your own purpose rather than the Lord. The only way to prevent this is to stay in prayer and in the word of God so that your motives remain pure as you serve. For me I have always found the sign that I am losing focus on why I'm serving to be my emotional state. By that I mean, when I find myself seeking to be fulfilled by the service rather than finding my fulfillment in God first, I know I am off track. I enjoy writing and it can be easy for me to find my purpose in writing to display whatever talent I feel I have through it. When I am writing to relay what God has put on my heart without trying to make the message or the information too complex or flashy then I am serving his purpose through the talent he has given. If I find myself trying to add concepts and personal thoughts that branch off from what he has placed on my heart, I am then trying to serve my purpose with the talent he has given. This is a daily awareness required because many times what God is speaking isn't flashy or going to get the claps from the people. Many times, we desire those things from people when we display our gifts or talents. This is the draw our flesh seeks from a fallen nature. Many have this mind when entering a covenant with a person. This is what fuels unhappiness, the expectation of someone fulfilling us emotionally, mentally, and physically. If they miss the mark at any time, it frustrates their idolatry. Instead of pointing to themselves concerning the idolatry they point to the person that's failing as their self-appointed God. This idolization towards others is normal in our worldly culture that doesn't desire love of another person without benefiting directly. It must be exposed and rejected. Only then can clarity exist in how to love someone.

Oneness guidelines

Doing the Lord's will is vital. It is the Lords will that if you enter marriage, you are to become one flesh with this person. **So be sure the one you are already one with is Christ first.** This will prevent you from being the one that brings any form of darkness to another. Remember that individual you are marrying is loved by God much greater than any emotion you could feel for them. Do right by them. God's covenant is not to be trampled upon because of a strong lustful desire for a person. It is written that the one who cannot control themselves, that one should marry rather than to burn with desire. Be not confused by this. Understand that the goal of each person is to live righteously. If you find intimate desire towards a woman as a man, then to marry her is the righteous thing to do as opposed to engaging in a sexual relationship outside of marriage. With that said the writer is not giving a guideline of marriage to be your sexual desire. The emphasis is simply exposing the seriousness of sexual desire. The priority in our lives is to cast that desire aside. To seek oneness with Christ first, then your oneness with your spouse will have the right foundation. So be clear of your intentions when meeting that person. Be sure they do the same. Becoming one with another person means in thought and action. You both must have the same desire for God in his word before joining each other in a covenant under God. God hates divorce. Many see this as a legal transaction of breaking up the marriage. I feel God is speaking to a much deeper purpose. He hates a household claiming his covenant but living divided amongst each other. Malachi 2:16 "For I hate divorce!" says the LORD, the God of Israel. "To divorce your wife is to overwhelm her with cruelty," says the LORD of Heaven's Armies. "So, guard your heart; do not be unfaithful to your wife. "For your wife my son, and your husband's my daughters may come with their own desires and wants. Those desires and wants cannot be a priority if they are not to love, respect and honor God. Neither can your own! Having stated this, please receive these words. Your marriage will do well if you both understand your purpose here on earth as it pertains to God. You both are secondary to Christ. Nothing and no-one in life comes before Christ, so be careful when choosing a spouse if you choose. Consider the cost and the error of bringing someone into your life that you have not built the right spiritual foundation with. To endure the wrong woman my son amongst your presence is to stand on the ledge of a bridge with your eyes closed. Solomon wrote in Proverbs 21:19 that it be better to live in a desert than with a nagging wife. Be sure my son with your conduct that she has words that respect you. Meaning live a respectful life towards her and others. Ensure you make peace rather than utter words of conflict. She is called to respect you by the word of God, and you are called to love her. These are not negotiable. The same for you, my daughters. If you choose a husband, have respect for him. It is not your duty to correct him with contempt or inform him of his shortcomings. Marry a man! A man of God that values the Lords words and leads in action in what it says. One that desires to protect you and provide for the household. Pray for him and encourage him in the word of God. Trust God to reveal such things to him that need correcting. It is your conduct that may aid that process. If you choose to be with him then that choice shows you accepting him as your head. Choose wisely. For a woman to marry an undisciplined man without integrity in the word of God is for her to pour acid to the top of her head. She will endure the pain as it slowly runs down her face, burning and scarring every inch it encounters. Remember to love and respect each other with grace and mercy. You are not here for yourself, but Christ. So, encourage each other in love to keep seeking him. Put away simple arguments on what preferences you have. You have denied yourself in following Christ. **What part of denying yourself still seeks preference?** Learn to live humbly and modestly. This is required whether you are single or married. Doing these things in a marriage is your form of worship to The Father for it shows respect for his order. Family is important and requires discipline and order, so everyone understands why they are here. Seek how to love purely as it is written to do so. Why be engaged to error? Error is never pleased or satisfied. Lastly, understand this, **marriage is not mandatory for your life.** It is a **choice**. Choose concerning God and not rush this decision but examine it with clarity. Many live in deep regret because of unmeasurable difficulties and challenges due to a lack of understanding concerning this decision. A man and a woman that seek to honor and please God in their marriage will do well even if they marry quickly. Whereas a man and woman seeking their own desires in a marriage will always find conflict within it. This will exist regardless of how long they have known each other or have been married. So, understand the necessity here.

Our lives reveal our loyalty

Exodus 20:3

"Thou shalt have no other gods before me."

Everything challenges something. The flesh challenges the spirit, anger challenges peace, lies challenge the truth, confusion challenges understanding, and hatred challenges love. Let not your heart be weary because there is a challenger to our Lord Jesus Christ. For there to be a challenger means there is something greater to oppose. It is only a challenge for the challenger, hence the term. The challenger only serves as an option for those not interested in the champion. This world and its desires to live in opposition to God reminds me of how fans are in sports. Many times, fans cheer for a challenger to upset a champion, but soon as the champion defeats the challenger they scatter without loyalty. Their hope in the challenge was just based on their hatred of the champion. This reminds me of this generation. The world hates Christ, the truth, and the Bible. Yet, if you ask those same people that hate the Bible about following Satan, many if not all will say no emphatically! See, they are not a fan of Satan but rather hate Christ and the truth because of what he represents. So, the ideas of Satan be what they rather align with all the while claiming to not align themselves with who those values align. This is a great deception. The reason many never see this deception is because they believe Satan to be an abstract idea and not one that is carried from within. This shows the importance of knowing God the Father through Christ Yeshua. The Christ stated this in **John 10:30. I and the Father are one.** Now take note of what happened after Yeshua stated this. It revealed the loyalty of the men of that time and in our generation currently. It says his Jewish opponents picked up stones to stone him as they felt that was blasphemy. If you do not believe your Heavenly Father desires to be one with you, literally dwelling in you then you do not know the Father. Is it not written that upon our belief in his son he would send us his Holy Spirit? There are times this is spoken of like an idea that we carry on a leash. No! The Holy Spirit was sent to dwell in us. Aren't we to be one with the Spirit that is in us? So, if the Spirit that dwells in us is Holy, what manner of life should we only be able to live? I ask these questions to reveal the true manner of each person. Your life and how you live it reveals what Spirit is in you.

Satan does not need you to be his fan, but rather a life that simply does not agree with Christ. The very Spirit of rebellion is found within mankind. The values and ways of the world show what Spirit dwells within it. With that said, it does not matter what Spirit you claim, your very life bears witness to the Spirit that dwells within you. The Spirit of Satan has already been defeated so he isn't challenging anything of God. That Spirit rather is looking to take as many with him to where he is going. Some look to the world and see many things happening that don't align with God's truth. So, in fear of standing up for God's truth they align with who they perceive is the champion, the safe pick that everyone is cheering for. On judgment day they will see a defeated challenger and realize the truth. Satan was never a champion. In his great fall, he lost his very self. His desire is for you to be lost also. For you to be blind also. For many Christians it's to think you are on God's team while cheering for the one that rejects him. For non-believers it is the belief that his way is better than God's way. Be not deceived, this wicked Spirit has been invoking the idea of God to many while rejecting the one true God. With all of this said, remember this. Your team is who you are **loyal** to. The one that you stand with regardless of the appearance of defeat. The one you are not ashamed to proclaim to everyone! The one you support through it all. I always see sports fans dressed in the teams' apparel whether it be their house hanging a flag or their car with a bumper sticker. Sadly, many have this form of loyalty to sports teams more than they do to Christ. You will find thousands of people pack a stadium to scream and cheer men and woman they have never had dinner with to score a basket or goal. Then you take those same people and have them attend a church service and they have difficulty with praise and worshiping God. The reservation to raise our hands and stretch out our arms never comes when cheering in sports. I seriously was one of these individuals at one point. Completely in love with sports fandom and very nonchalant towards worship. This amongst many other sorts of examples show our lostness without Christ truth in us. It also displays the very carnal mind we can slip into. Make no mistake about this. What you proclaim from the mountain top is what you love. What you are not ashamed of is where your loyalty resides. Each of us reveals what team we are truly on.

Each of us proclaims that team from the mountaintops with our lives. As we examine our lives, may there be godly sorrow within if we see anything that brings forth such thankfulness and loyalty, such cheer and celebration while absent concerning our Lord. Be not deceived, where you find loyalty, you find respect. Where you find respect, you find honor. The Father will never forget his commandments. It's time we remember.

Why Christ was and is mandatory

Many cannot find loyalty to Christ because they really have no idea why he was sent. Really important to get this. Many hear that Jesus died for them and it sounds like the greatest display of love any of us could ever fathom. That's because it is, but how would a believer explain the why behind this to a non-believer? Let alone to one claiming to believe that doesn't truly understand this but is too afraid to say so. The first aspect of this is to understand that the world is under a curse. That curse was issued from the creator of the universe due to the rebellion of our original flesh parents Adam and Eve. This curse is death and death eternally. Now, while under this curse mankind has brought many forms of living that were driven by man's personal desires. Because those desires spread sin like wildfire upon the earth, a lost nature of living begin to become the normal for mankind. It is God that provided his chosen people instruction on how sin could be temporarily covered. That instruction was that a sacrifice was required yearly by the high priest. This sounds odd I'm sure to the casual person foreign to biblical context that may be reading this so I will explain. Sin is the opposite of God who is pure and righteous without stain or blemish. When his creation sinned, the opposite of God entered the world. To better clarify, I say this. God is living and there is no death in him. So, when sin was done by man which is the opposite of God, the opposite of life naturally was the result. In the Father's perfect Holy existence, a simple apology cannot cover such an alteration to his creation's purpose. No, what is pure and blameless must die to cover such a cosmic altering of his creation. There is a severe cost that is to be paid for such a thing done towards him. For sin is ultimately like playing Russian roulette with a full chamber. We have just been conditioned by the liar that the bullets have no effect because we get to keep pulling the trigger, albeit wounded after every shot, but I digress. In God's perfect plan he provided a foreshadowing for his people whom he made a covenant with. He gave instructions on how they might have their sins atoned for every year. He put a structure in place where the people had a high priest, and he would present a sacrifice on their behalf. This was to prepare the world for his plan of providing that pure, blameless sacrifice from a high priest that would cover sins for eternity. For the high priest would be the sacrifice himself. That's right! An actual Holy life in the flesh. You see, God is just, meaning he does not delight in watching the guilty go free. Despite what many claim God's grace is, it is not that. In his just ways he delights in seeing the rightful punishment for the crime committed. **We committed sin so death must take place as the just punishment.** That's where we see the unmatched priceless gift given through Christ Jesus. That curse of death not only was taken upon his shoulders in the flesh but taken for all. See to sin is to say to God I don't want what you are. I choose the opposite of you. When sin takes place so does death because sin is not of God, and neither is death. So, doing the opposite of God produces the opposite of him just to clarify that point further.

God who is life and is love understands our rejection of him to be a rejection of those two things. To be with God, there must be a turn from this choice. Many don't see their rejection of God as a rejection of life and love. This is unfortunate to say the least. Without knowledge of this, they don't understand what is required to make their existence right with God. For once the truth entered the world and that truth was rejected and killed, God used the man that lived purely in truth as the sacrifice for those that would believe in him. We know that man to be Yeshua from Nazareth. For those that rejected him, rejected the miracles done through him. They rejected his teachings and criticized his life because he engaged with the people disregarded by those who had religious power. This rejection was extreme to the degree that they arrested him and found him guilty of blasphemy. Blasphemy in this case was Yeshua the Mashiach claiming to be God. Yet if these men had read the scriptures with an open heart, they would have known that the very man God would send to be their King and savior was upon them. So, in the ultimate just decision from God, he uses everyone's non-belief concerning his son Yeshua as their judgment. **For there is no other name in heaven or on earth that can save anyone from the fate of the world.** In this we see a love so just and so pure that the world still cannot comprehend it fully. For those who do not desire this truth or feel it is nothing more than fables to create fear. Please think about this. Who on earth is promising your life to be eternal? Examine where the idea of rejecting Christ came from and why you have such confidence in it. Has anyone convinced you that death is not certain? Do you see a world with evil in it? Once you can answer these basic questions honestly you have a decision to make. Are you willing to chance your entire existence on a world with evil in it that has death daily? All of this is because of the mere understanding that you want to live how you choose. The choice is yours to make. The love and life through Christ are for your receiving. Just the same, sin and death is also yours for the receiving. It is you that shall reap what you desire. The requirement to save us has been given through a man of integrity and love. A man of truth and compassion. Think not that rejecting such a man is taken lightly by the father. For the father loves him deeply, for it is his son. He sent him for you, so that you might know the truth and might value such a love that has no comparison. All the while lives are rejecting him for temporary pleasure. It will not be God's absence of love or desire for any of us that will bring forth judgement. Rather our very lack of love and desire towards him will bring forth a just punishment. I do not have any words greater than these in hopes to compel you to run towards his open arms. For there will come a day when you will not be able to.

Freedom in Yeshua is victorious

There is an aspect of living in Christ that gets manipulated by some but valued by others. That is the freedom in Christ. It is truly unlike anything the world can comprehend. The world cannot even speak of it, for it cannot speak the truth. Once you receive the truth, you shall be free from all the ways of the world. You no longer exist with this subconscious desire to do what you have been shown by the world. No longer enslaved to the ideas, the words, and the traditions of the world. This freedom Christ speaks of is what the evil one desires us to never receive. That deceiving devil is willing to kill or silence anyone with this freedom. The fear Satan has is that this freedom will be desired after being heard by the world. How do I know this? Let's take into consideration what history has shown us. Since documented in the Bible and considering this very day we see a consistent manner of how Christians are treated. Many killed in the Eastern world for simply speaking about Jesus. Here in the Western world the attempt is to silence all who have this freedom in Christ, especially if you try to inform others of it. This is just referring to information. These are the extremes being taken by the world because of information alone. It is because the world has a Spirit of rebellion and hatred towards the truth.

Lies keep people in bondage and the prince of the air desires all to be in bondage to him. How else can he control everyone? This is why it is important to beware of wolves in sheep's clothing. Anyone in position to present the gospel falsely is in position to rob people of their freedom. Paul informed the **Galatians this in Chapter 5:13** For you were called to freedom, brothers, *and sisters;* only *do* not *turn* your freedom into an opportunity for the flesh but serve one another through love. Meaning your freedom is not to be used as some life pass to carry out personal desires for yourself. No, it is to serve others through love.

This freedom in Christ grants peace the world cannot understand as it has **nothing** to do with their ways or things. This is not profitable to a Satanic system that needs everyone to live blindly on how good their lives are or could be based on what they have. That's the plan of the evil one. **To have everyone follow him and convince everyone that following their own preferences, their own knowledge, and their own desires to be something unique to them.** Everyone by the end of their life followed someone. You either followed Satan (your own way of thinking) and his ways or you followed Christ and his. To all whom may ever read this. Please take caution and understand. There is nothing in this world that can satisfy your soul. You can chase them and attain them all to find out it satisfies nothing more than your flesh, for a moment. To satisfy the flesh is to disregard the spirit. They will always clash. The flesh seeks to attain worldly things and the spirit seeks heavenly things. The Father knows of your needs and is not against you. We on the other hand are against him. So, seek him first my brothers and sisters, my children and any that will ever read this. Seek him first! Don't you know

he will add all things to you?! Do you think anything is

too hard for the creator of the universe? If these

questions appear to rattle your understanding of God,

my hope is that you might desire to know him. For yes

indeed he is good! Spiritual freedom only comes by

way of Christ who has asked the Father to send his

Holy Spirit for us. This is to be our desire while here

on this planet. We are not permanent residents here,

but merely foreigners passing through. We are not to

desire the things those that love this world do. The

only way your focus is on your flesh desires is if you

truly disregard the spirit. Be not deceived, this is true

and there is no victory in such a life that has such a

focus. The only victory is in the truth with Christ.

_____

(shishi) יְ שִׁ שִׁ

<u>**Righteous self-control**</u>

This chapter will not only speak to the strength that comes with self-control but also how it is near and dear to me. This fruit of the Spirit is one that I am very thankful God continues to help me with. It is one that I have had the most difficulty in this life. You see, self-control requires respect and honor towards God. An honoring of the Holy Spirit as it speaks to you louder than any given moment that can arise in this life. I am speaking to moments that may mentally or physically feel good to the flesh. At that moment you must understand that you are being lied to from within. Yes, your mind is conflicting with the spirit. Forgetfulness is so easy. All that is required is a simple disregard of what is known to be spiritually good for you. No-one can remember this for you and no-one that does for themselves does so in their own power. This is a fruit of the Spirit. The Holy Spirit gives us the ability to show self-control. I tell you the truth, the result of not exercising self-control is one that could alter your very life. Yes, it is that serious, and a choice made without self-control will be reflected upon with great confusion, frustration, sadness, and for me a great deal of guilt. Trust our Father my brothers and sisters in Christ. The true Father God in Heaven. Trust him. He is pure light and love. Self-control is a strength and a peace very rarely found. For it is a daily, weekly, dare I say hourly job that requires discipline. Honor such work with diligence, for one day used without self-control can affect the remaining. Many like me are living in frustration or in direct consequences from choices they made years ago without self-control. Many times, that choice was only 10 minutes of their day. So, discipline yourself, as the result has a great benefit to your life. This is only done through consistent efforts to keep your thoughts on Christ. You do this by reading his words and putting it into practice.

Recognize sin as death described in God's word. Acknowledge what is of God and what he says is good for you. Many rely on their upbringing to create their basis for what is good and what is not. This is because God who is the great light, created goodness and righteousness to be passed down as an understanding, but so did evil and wickedness. The family is where all children were to get an up close and true depiction of how-to live-in Christ. Unfortunately, that depiction has come to be with very little self-control and many times claiming to be of Christ. Now in these days the traditions of the family mostly come from the world. Such as holidays, festivals, parades, lifestyles, etc.... The confusion of many comes when they see Christians participating in the **same things** the people in the world are participating in. I can understand how that is confusing. It really doesn't make any sense seeing as though we as Christians see those in the world as lost. **So, if they are lost, and we do the things they do while claiming Christ how much more lost are we?** Your self-control to not partake in these traditions does not make you a Jehovah witness or some other extreme sect of Christianity. It doesn't scream to anyone I'm better than you such as the Hebrew Israelites do at people. You do not have to align yourself with these extreme groups to have the righteous self-control Christ desires for us. For some this will be difficult of course. Many relatives and friends, let alone coworkers and church members all delight themselves in participating in the traditions of the world. To interact with them can be challenging while they decide to dress up for Halloween or put up their Yule tree for Christmas. It's because they are using their freedom in Christ to indulge the flesh. To watch such behavior can be difficult because it serves no purpose. There are literally pagans that put trees up at the end of the year and decorate them just like many Christians do. There are literal Satan worshipers that dress up for Halloween just like many Christians do. So, no one can make since of such traditions being adopted by Christians. It is simply a distorted view of the freedom Christ came to give. Those true to the faith will respect your decision to not be a part of the traditions of the world. Those that are slave to the world still, will be offended by you. We ought to respect brothers and sisters in Christ that choose to not participate as we are called to live peaceably with all man. With that said don't dress pagan origins as honoring Christ. Even evil doesn't try and do that. They honor what is their own, we should honor what is ours.

Do not let the world corrupt you

Please understand that you can always give to others throughout the year, let alone during the end of it if you desire without observing the traditions of the world. They all breed hypocrisy. They all are self-serving ways to please the flesh. Understand the holidays of your culture here in America are not from God but are rather from people that have origins of pagan worship. They are used for flesh indulgence. You are not to live as the pagans do or practice their ways. Let alone claim to honor the one true God with their traditions. **This is very important!** I have heard many people defend these traditions with very warped thinking. Sayings like it's fun, it brings me joy, or it brings me peace. The flesh is easily manipulated through feelings and the appearance of these things. Resist any temptation to invest your money or time into these wicked celebrations masking themselves to honor God. Some of which don't even attempt to hide the demonic influence. As for Christmas, what a wonderful thing to remember the birth of our Lord. Be not deceived though no-one knows the birthday of Jesus Christ nor were we commanded to celebrate it by gifting each other materialistic things for ourselves or others. This is manipulation and cruel in my opinion for the sake of capitalism to put Christ at the center of such a tradition. I speak about this one holiday in specific not because of my personal opinion. Rather the historical facts show that Christ name is being used to align a pagan holiday to his followers. It is astounding to see so many things corrupted by this world. If anyone wants to simply indulge in materialism, then do so without trying to claim you are honoring Jesus by doing it. It was not challenging to find traditions that were upheld by the catholic church. One that should be acknowledged was Saturnalia. Once you find this you will then see how those claiming Christ with political power came to a compromise with that entity to incorporate this holiday. There is no secret to how the date came to be, to so call honor our Lord. I tell you the truth. The very Christianity we know that is so intertwined with that Catholic church shows the corruption that entered it. It was bound to take place when a pagan claimed to see a sign and made our belief the religion of that culture. They did not want to let go of the very pagan practices and beliefs they had. **So, they did the most wicked thing possible. They merged the two together as a compromise.** God didn't send Christ to compromise with Gentiles to say the least. He didn't even compromise with the very Jews he led out of slavery. So take that as proof he is not for traditions created by the world.

You must <u>first</u> deny yourself

This all comes back to the necessity of denying ourselves daily because everyone participates in these sorts of traditions blindly. I remember asking my nephew if he wanted to know where this holiday started, and he said no. I asked why? He essentially informed me that he enjoys it. This is common practice and is disturbing. When my delight in a thing is more important than the truth, I display a lack of self-control. We cannot simply make what we enjoy into a form of righteousness to try and justify our enjoyment. God decides that. I can recall when a famous rapper by the name of Biggie Smalls decided to start a clothing line. This wasn't uncommon for celebrities at that time nor is it now. What was uncommon was the decision he made on what to call it. The name of his clothing line was going to be 666. Before it was able to be released, he was gunned down in a drive by and lost his life at age 24. For many young people the potential of walking around with 666 on their shirts was going to be a reality. See many people do not care what is truly right nor do they care about the origins of what they practice. This is why denying yourself is so essential, for yes it partners with self-control. This was and currently is the area that tries to creep up and cause division with me. **The desire to make a case for myself concerning a matter that involves me.** It must die daily within me. For it is a hungry lion desiring to consume me constantly. I once heard a pastor ask, how does a person that has died to Christ have so many preferences? That question left me dumbfounded. Yet many have never really considered this as I hadn't. Doesn't this show our lack of righteous self-control? An obvious rhetorical question for it clearly does. Understand this, the world teaches us to live without regard for restrictions. As a follower of Christ, we are very much in a life of restriction. Is not this concerning the desires of the flesh? Aren't we all reading the same Holy Bible? Following the same teachings of the same man Jesus Christ? It is truly impossible to believe we are. What truly separates us from the world? If we are free to live how we choose in the freedom of Christ how can we tell a world already doing such that they are in error. That would be hypocrisy and hypocrisy is not of God but the evil one. Trust me here. Wherever you find hypocrisy there you will find Satan and his demons. We have confessed to believe by claiming Jesus as Lord, but do we understand what belief even is? The Hebrew root word for belief is **Emunah**. It speaks to one's life of faithfulness. **So, believing must mean the act of living out what you have proclaimed with your mouth.** Again, he informed us to **first deny ourselves**, then **carry our cross**, then **follow him.** If carrying your cross shows up for you as the frustrations of your family or friends talking behind your back because you think you're holier than thou, because you no longer do what they do. Understand Christ said you are blessed when this happens to you. How will you endure such talking about you without denying yourself? You will not endure it at all but rather find offence towards them and your behavior will not align with Christ. If the world condemns or persecutes you, then praise God for it. For he said the kingdom of heaven is yours! How will you endure such harsh treatment without denying yourself? You will not, for you will take it personal and make the gospel your weapon to condemn others and your life will not align with Christ. We must endure with understanding. **Denying ourselves is the starting point that enables carrying our cross and following Jesus possible.**

With all of this said, don't let the world corrupt you. You can enjoy life in its abundance in Christ without walking on eggshells or doing what everyone does. **If we profess to be saved through the blood of Christ which came from him giving his body, then our lives ought to be lived like we remember that.** Our lives should reflect his sacrifice to others. Living that life should be with a daily remembrance. As common as eating and drinking. What if we started observing communion with that sort of understanding more than sipping some grape juice and eating a cracker? What does all of this have to do with righteous self-control you may ask. Well to put it plainly, to live the gospel without mixing in the ways of the world requires righteous self-control. It will not be some walk in the park to start but over time by the grace of God you will find more peace and a better balance to your life. Man has a form of self-control that is not righteous. Rather it appears on the surface as such but inwardly it lusts after the very things they are to stay away from. In secret or in the dark you can say they indulge, and great is their indulgence!

Tools used for bondage

This is the sorrow of the truth. You will find that the evil that runs this world has its hands in all things here. With that said, understand this. You cannot be controlled by the ways of this world unless you give it permission. You give it power by thinking like them and doing the things they do. I can only speak about how I granted the world power over my life. I believe many have experienced or are experiencing these chains. I hope to shed light on these chains as they have been glorified as good by the evil one. Posing as potential good things to our very flesh but are the tools the devil uses to destroy us. **These chains will come in the form of fear, finances, identity confusion, purpose disruption, mental and emotional instability, and entertainment.** These things plus much more alike them will come in various ways to alter your focus off Christ. Not only that but they are intended to have us never even consider Christ. Exposing these for what they are is essential for many are chained and enslaved by them. Ironically enough, thinking they grant freedom. I must speak to each one as this is how I nearly ruined my life and disregarded my birthright. So, let's speak to each one starting with the spirit God does **not** give, **fear.**

Fear

This is the basis of the entire world. Everyone has dealt with fear. So much so we accept it as a part of our norm. This world does not understand that the

Father did not give the spirit of fear as it is written. **Through sin fear came, because the origin of fear comes from an acknowledgment of disobedience and an expectation for a consequence.** There-fore the evil one uses this as a tool to shackle many. Now, I am not talking about sensible caution. For many can confuse sensible caution as fear. There is no fear required to not go lay on railroad tracks. Some would try this to display mindless fun. The one that does not do such foolishness isn't afraid of trains or being hit by one. He is simply practicing sensible caution and not testing God by putting himself in harm's way. So, the fear I speak of is the fear of death and the truth. Every sinful action tries to reject the notion of judgement, because sin alarms the sinner initially of fear. Fear of consequences. This is why criminals do not turn themselves in once they commit the crime. They run and hide in fear of punishment, or they lie to cover what they have done. This took place in the

garden of Eden with Adam and Eve. They

immediately hid themselves the moment they sinned.

Fear had now entered the world through disobedience.

The one that uses fear here on earth is the one that

knows God's judgement is coming upon this

world. He cannot escape it, so he tries to use it to his

advantage.

Fear is joined by hatred. In this generation you see

many living in lifestyles of lust that promote pride.

There is a deep level of hatred residing within such a

lifestyle. Hatred of self and others. The reason pride is

necessary for them is because it is the very character

trait that keeps God away. They need God away from

them so their conscience can ignore the fear of

judgement. For you shall hear of phobias across the

planet. This is not by accident. Those living in fear of

judgement desire to place such a title upon those who remind them of such judgement that shall come from God. It is a psychological play to invert their feelings onto those they hate. Be not baited into offence when such terms like phobias are used to describe those who know the truth concerning lustful lifestyles. There will be judgement from God concerning homosexuality. There will be judgement from God concerning the way children have been manipulated and confused about their birth identities. This all has come from a wicked spirit of lust that hates everyone. It does not want children to be born and if they are born it desires to corrupt them. This is a spiritual war against the God ordained family structure. Don't be confused about this. This is all about hatred of God. When someone hates you deeply, they desire to ruin everything associated with you. Starting with your identity, then with those that cannot defend themselves. The evil one fears the power of God in Christ. A family with Christ as the head, which has one man (husband) and one woman (wife) whom have children walking in righteousness. This destroys the gates of hell for it cannot touch such a family. This is what the evil spirit of that lifestyle fears. Nothing can touch that family for the one true God in Christ watches over that household!

Now there is another fear that exists. That would be the cowards of the world. Because of such people many sinful acts have been excused. Many wicked deeds have been ignored. Some examples of such look like this. A congregation that sits and allows a preacher to stand in front of hundreds and speak a word not found in scripture and no-one speaks up during it to denounce its lies. The fear of public opinion even when you know the truth of God is being dishonored. This is happening outside of the church as well. Many live as cowards concerning children. Staying silent as young people are being informed of confusion about their identities. If this wasn't bad enough. It's to the extreme that parents are allowing children to have surgeries to alter their appearance and take drugs to alter their natural functions. What a disgraceful spirit this is!! No wonder the father plans to cast cowards first into the lake of fire. See Revelations 21:8. No-one is above reproach. Fear is what people use to dismiss sinful behaviors such as sexual immorality within families like molestation or rapes. Fear of embarrassment or of shame that such a darkness exists amongst them. Fear prevents the abused from often seeking help. Fear also promotes cowardness that is found within the abuser who hides his actions. Fear can alter a person's voice, cause trembling, and often cause a complete shutdown in front of others. Many question the Bible due to the fear of what others may say or perceive about them if they hold firm to its doctrines. This has caused many to denounce Christ with their lives in front of those content living in sin. As you can see, fear is a spirit intended to place shackles upon the soul. It is written in **Hebrews 2:15 that Jesus came to free the captives, all who had the fear of death.** It is only through him that this spirit can be conquered. Many will deny the very existence of God to soothe their fear of death mentally. Many will keep themselves busy in life to avoid the reality that this very life is short lived. There are several things' people do to avoid this reality in life and it's because the fear of it can be all consuming without Christ as Lord in your life. Trust in Christ and prepare yourself with self-control knowing that your father is with you always and did not give this spirit.

Finances

This is an area that is not really considered by many as a tool of the devil. Yet the more people you speak with the more you hear of this being an area of difficulty and worry. Anytime anything becomes a focal point in your life that is not God it becomes an idol. Again, remember these tools from Satan are intended to keep you distracted from walking with Christ. To be in debt is to owe a thing to someone or an institution, typically a financial obligation that has been agreed upon. Simply honor your commitment. Do not allow such a temporal thing like money to cause you stress or anxiety. Wherever you find stress and anxiety you find one that is lacking trust in Christ. When you start to stress over things of this world you open yourself up to burdens and typically people place their burdens on others. Many times, without even trying. Think of it this way. Whatever you are not taking care of will become the unkept things another will observe. This has the potential to bring burdens to others. It is written to not be a burden to anyone. Debts bring burdens to yourself and others as well. I have lived with poor accountability in my life concerning finances. Once I met my wife this burden was placed upon her, and it had deeply negative effects on our marriage. There is no mercy with debt, and it will follow generations after you if you do not put God over it. By that I mean have integrity with your finances. Be a steward of what God has given you. Be thankful for what you do have and stop striving in this life for things. Did our Lord not ask "is not life more than food and the body more than clothes? Our Lord Jesus Christ was trying to get our focus on what's most important. The Holy Spirit is here to remind us of what he said. So, remember this!

Keep yourself away from the thoughts of quick cash. Understand you have exactly what you should and lack nothing. This is true regardless of your financial state. **A very good rule of thumb I have had to learn is this. If you aren't disciplined to save money, you aren't disciplined enough to pay it back.** Don't deceive yourself, saving money is paying yourself. If you can't be diligent to pay yourself, why would you even consider paying someone else what you owe? Being diligent with your money honors the one whom has blessed you with it. How can you give to others while in debt? Even if you were to give, the debt creates an inability to be joyful in your giving. God loves a cheerful giver. Not one giving resentfully because of self-created financial challenges. Or the idea that he can be manipulated to grant you more of what you are not stewarding well.

Understand this concerning education as it pertains to debt. Gaining education for the purpose of seeking a career is not a bad thing. Gaining education for the purpose of seeking status is a despicable thing. Understand it will cost you either way, so have a plan. Ensure your intent for acquiring this debt is not for social status. You can honor God with your career, while trying to honor God with your status is like chasing the wind. It's just not possible as he doesn't care about social status and how the world perceives it as relevant. Let the one that can receive this, receive it.

Finances will always be an area of life that reflects a person's integrity. You can tell what matters to a person by how they spend their money. What they use it on. Life will always come down to choices. The best choice comes from the guidance of God. Second guess nothing as your initial decision should not be a guess. What it should be rather, is one made after careful prayer in the spirit. God knows how to inform his own when something is not his will for them. Trust that and let no one distort his voice for you, but never think you know his voice if you aren't in his word regularly. Further-more be at peace, yes peace. Do not let finances distract you or alter your character from a place of thankfulness. Pay back what you owe, by doing this you will display your integrity in the Lord. It has taken me all of 40 years to understand this concept. **God desires to be Lord in every aspect of your life.**

Identity-confusion

This is one of the most manipulated ways the world can trap you. It usually is attacked during your youth so please read with understanding. If it is the Lord's will, I hope to be here for all my children's youth and adulthood. If they choose to have children, my grandchildren's youth as well. Read this and perceive it fully. You must know who you are in Christ. You are not a sexual attraction or a race, you are not your talents or your skills. You are a soul from God. God desires you to be his child and for you to live forever with him. **This only takes place with a spiritual birth in him through his son Jesus Christ**. That is your identity if you desire it! You must choose to inherit what has been laid up for you. There is no inheritance to all these things the world wants you to stake claim to, but death. The inheritance of a child of God is life. Do not let the world convince you that their identities don't lead to death. The world desires you to wear them pridefully. Not until this country America introduced it, did the color of your skin become a way to classify people. Now this generation desires to classify people by their sexual attraction and cannot reconcile what differentiates a man from a woman. No-one can blame the country for this nonsense though. This is mankind's depraved mind that has rejected God and now is committed to ignorance and foolishness. People have always been classified by the region or land in which they lived. That is all. The sickness of mankind can't help but to focus on the appearance of people. So, they began to call each other white or black. Referring to the skin tone of a person in hopes to feel superior. Apparently, it is now the blacks turn to play this game. While both reside in the same land as Americans. What a truly sad situation, but this is what happens when you do not have your identity in Christ. You are always seeking the approval of others or seeking to lift yourself above others. Know who you are and do not partake in this sickness!

Truth is with the light, which is the Father in Heaven

with his son Christ. Through your choices to align

your mind with truth and love in Christ, you will live

forever in God. After your flesh departs, what's left is

the invisible inside of you. Your thoughts and your

beliefs. Your true motives and intentions for living.

Keep these clean with the right food and liquid. That

food is the belief that Christ gave his body as a

sacrifice for you. That his bloodshed is for the sins we

committed not his own. This was done out of his love

for us and was required so that they be forgiven. That

same body rose from the dead showing that death

has no power over Him or any that believe in Him.

Have no confusion about who you are, for the very

son of God gave his life for you to know who you are.

For yes, the world has its self-imposed version of the

truth created by them. They hate Yeshua the Christ

as it is written, so they will hate you too if you walk in

truth. The truth is above this world and its traditions, false holidays, and those living in their false identities boasting in false love and pride. You need not judge it for it has already been judged. They judge themselves by how their conduct is displayed. The lifestyles of those in opposition to the word of God always is exposed as hypocritical and self-centered. Simply refrain yourself from such lifestyles and if anybody asks what religion you follow, simply say you are from the light and believe in the teachings and life of Yeshua the Christ. **Know who you are.** You will be made to feel less than, this is because people only choose to follow what the world says. It's easier for them because following the world doesn't conflict with the flesh. Sadly, this was a past of mine also. As dysfunctional as this sounds, my life was easier when I didn't care about it. When I lived recklessly without regard of God, without morals and integrity I was able to commit sin without concern for what is right. It took

nothing of me to live in the world, just my self-

centered pride. Now consider that my life was in

shambles, financially, emotionally, and mentally. Yet

that was the easy life. Many live the easy life very

aware that everything is in shambles but never think it

isn't what God desires for them. This is the world;

they use celebrities and entertainment to push the

easy life. We meet friends and colleagues that are

actively living an easy life and we desire it. Yet we

see what they present is not healthy nor does it

produce joy and peace. It often gets ignored because

of the false presentation of happiness. The false idea

that there is actual freedom in living apart from God.

With that said, in Christ you have a strong defense of

what they don't know. Although their conscience is

already aware of the law of God. What they hate is

whatever is done to them, so they know what not to

do to others. Do not argue about anything with such people. Offer what is Holy to those who seek holiness. Let righteousness clothe you in every encounter. As it is written, do not cast your pearls to the pigs or they will be trampled upon, and they may turn to tear you apart. You will know who wishes to receive the gospel and who is of this world, demonic and wicked in all their thoughts. So be wise. Your identity is sealed if you abide in this truth, and no-one can take you out of the hand of Christ. So, remember your very identity is significant to our Lord, for he gave his life that you might know it!

Purpose Disruption

The heart is more deceitful above all things and desperately sick, as it is written in **Jeremiah 17:9.** So what manner of love would tell a person to follow it? What purpose would someone have for you to give such advice? The Lord God tells us the condition of our hearts, that it is deceitful and sick. The world tells us follow that heart to find your purpose. So, let's examine what the world presents to us when people follow their hearts. The proof of what is true always reveals itself through how people live. If you turn on your television and watch an awards show or the red-carpet event prior to it, let alone a concert, you will see something amazingly open and appalling. It isn't the scandalously dressed women or the arrogantly vain men. It isn't the thousands of lights flashing from cameras to capture these people either that is the most appalling. Now all those things are very appalling and sick but what is even more sorrowful is the screaming young people who are standing around watching these events, some in tears or passing out from the excitement. The excitement of seeing the person they have been admiring. Now think about this.

How did a young life get to admire another person that deeply for singing a song or being in a movie? This is a clear idolization being glorified. Many parents have even encouraged such things by allowing their children to put pictures on their walls of these people. We allow them to watch movies that present violence, sex, and unhealthy lifestyles as what's popular. The influence being passed down to these young people is being carried out by individuals creating from their hearts. The young people are using their hearts to desire what they are influenced by.

The world presents the love of its kind. Not God's love. This will be very challenging because to recognize it brings scrutiny. Just remember to love everyone with the truth. The evil one has put a lot of effort into trying to separate the truth from love. Now we see a generation believing the truth and love to be whatever you decide for yourself. You can love a person and not agree with them or love their ways because a person can live a way of life that was not created by God. For God, The Father of Christ created all things good. He would not have said something was wrong and then wanted his people to condone it. Yet choices and actions, have always been given to man; so, brace yourself as we examine man's choice of the most celebrated and welcomed activity in the world. Sex. The evil one says sex should be explored upon. Yet according to the World Health Organization and the Pan American Health Organization, there are more than 30 different bacteria, viruses and parasites known to be transmitted through sexual contact. In 2021, 2.5 million cases were reported in the United States with about half coming from people ages 15-24. Around the world an estimated 374 million sexually transmitted infections occur each year. Now that is according to the CDC (center for disease control). Sexually transmitted diseases are considered a hidden epidemic because these numbers clearly are problematic in the world, yet sex remains glorified. What is also glorified is homosexuality, yet gay and bisexual men are disproportionately affected from all others according to these statistics. So, who is reading this and wondering if God was in error by telling us the sexual immoral (promiscuous heterosexuals included and those who practice homosexuality) will not inherit his kingdom? Who would want you to engage in something that plagues the world with disease? Surely not someone that truly loves you. These are the questions not being asked to our young people and their purpose in life is being disrupted!

We keep telling people God loves them despite the choices they make, and neglect to tell them their choices show no love for Him. When we neglect to tell the truth about our hearts it creates a belief that our purpose is now to fulfill the desires of that very heart and many times boast in it. For man wants answers to all things that conflict with his understanding. Even while not seeking a righteous spiritual life in Christ. So, man creates his version of the truth to satisfy his desires. By default, all of mankind wants truth, to the point it will create its own version when he disagrees with God. Understand the reason for purpose disruption from the evil one is to control you. The deception is that you will think your identity is unique, yet it will simply be following the identity the world is giving you. Your desire to create your own purpose can serve as a form of control over your life. Many will not allow anyone to disrupt it. Not their family, friends, coworkers, or any enemy against it. Your goals, your desires, your sorrow, your happiness, your money, your passions. **All can disrupt your actual purpose**. All are designed to replace your true purpose. For not many shall find the true path as it is a narrow road and can be fleshly lonely. How many understand your purpose is to suffer for Christ in this flesh? **Yes, to deny yourself is to suffer in the flesh.** Read **2 Timothy 3:12-13**. **In fact, everyone who wants to live a godly life in Christ Jesus will be persecuted, while evildoers and impostors will go from bad to worse, deceiving and being deceived.**

So, ask the Holy Spirit to strengthen you so you never forget to be fruitful in peace, love, and joy. The pure light will be with you and is your comforter. That uncomfortable feeling you may get when standing for the truth in Christ when people frown upon you is a result of living your true purpose. **Read 1 Peter 2:20-21.** There is a price for living in the truth with Christ and despite what evil in the church claims, it is not gaining wealth. **It is true suffering and at times discomfort for the truth**. Now suffering is obviously not a popular term when it comes to informing someone's purpose. Although this is not the most popular thing to present it aligns with the word of God. What is more received is what is not found in the word of God. So, you see why the latter is more desired, for there are more people interested in the world than the gospel. Christ informed us to consider the cost. The price we pay in this world while in this flesh for living in the truth cannot be a burden we complain about. Many turn away out of fear of receiving potential suffering or frustrations towards the challenges. As we endure, ask in Christ's name for a pure heart and clear understanding of your purpose. Then you shall receive it if you believe it without doubting. Then you will expect this and not be burdened. Glorifying God during the very persecution that comes! Finding contentment with what God has allotted you, instead of this striving to gain more and more of what you already have. If you find yourself without a single item to your name, you are still unable to claim you have nothing. God forbid you perceive the gift of salvation to be a waste. It is a privilege and an honor to live your life in Christ. To suffer in carrying one's own cross and denying the flesh daily is but a temporary burden to the flesh. A burden we must carry with joy for our Lord suffered for us, leaving an example, that we should follow in his steps. To this we were called. We ought to endure with passion for our purpose is to reflect Christ while temporarily here. Once you delight in this information, you will recognize your identity in Christ. Selah

Entertainment

I cannot stress the importance of guarding what enters your eyes, for this transmits to the mind and the mind is one with the heart. Be careful what enters your ears for these travel to the same mind. What we watch and what we listen to trains our mind on what secret images and voices we will entertain. These are very powerful tools that are used to connect with people all over the world. Now, remember the world hates Christ. Meaning his teachings, and ways. They prefer their own ways. The most popular way to display this is through entertainment. Since it is a tool to mask wickedness, it gives those that create it and consume it a feeling of escaping the truth. Using a mask of not being "real" or "just fun". Yet it's always real enough to display a visual to your eyes or real enough to be heard through your ears. Real enough to take up time in your day and bring forth emotions and devotion to it. In **Matthew 6:22, Yeshua the**

Christ was very clear about this. Whatsoever you put in your vision creates your darkness. What you allow inside of you through your senses is your agreement with its creation. It all travels to the mind. Everything is designed with the intent to be learned as it trains your mind to receive what is given. Be very careful of this! You may find yourself learning to train your mind in the wickedness that's been given. Even worse you will come to enjoy it and cling to it. Once you realize this truth, your eyes will be truly open to the bondage you have created for yourself.

Entertainment is vast and broad across the planet. **It plagues every nation as it masks itself with the harmless undertone of its just fun or it's not that serious**. The Father knows of this tool, this weapon. It's why he said no weapon formed against him shall prosper. Now many will say that the fame and the fortune gathered by those that indulge in this are experiencing a prosperous life. To that we should rebuke with scripture. So, what does it profit a man to gain the whole world and lose his soul? Those in these arts are not excluded from the same pains that afflict those working other jobs in the world. No amount of fame or fortune or talent or skill can cure the state of humanity. The state of humanity is in rebellion against what is true and pure and honest, and without hypocrisy. If you neglect the soul, it will show you what you are missing. If you satisfy the flesh it will hunger for more. The flesh has no limits, no gauge to be aware of. It is incapable of sensing when enough is enough until it's too late, and at times the person still cannot stop the desire to fulfill it. For entertainment is real. It's real for those that do it and for those that enjoy it. **Maintain self-control when it pertains to entertainment, or it will consume you**.

Train your body and value this temple. **It is the temple of God**.

Now I am not telling you that all entertainment is bad or wrong, but all things are not profitable to the soul. You must have the right mind to discern. Be on guard to not focus on judging these things or people, for even that can serve as a priority to some. Simply stay away from what is not for you. Many engage in the enjoyment of filthy entertainment that says and presents things that are obviously nonproductive to a healthy mind. Unfortunately, this may be presented to you through family, friends, associates, or co-workers. This can be challenging to deal with but keep it simple. Simply say "it's not for me" or "no thank you". The things I have written to you are all things I have dealt with myself. My children, I know in some form or fashion you will also. Use this please as a reference point. But first, measure it by the word of God. With all this said, simply be on guard. You are not here to live cavalier as if this life is just some moment in time that does not have consequences. Seek what is wise and put it into action in your life with Christ as your head.

Mental Instability

All the things listed here are designed to bring you to this place. The place the evil one wants everyone. For once you are in this place you are easily controlled and will not see clearly. Now let me first start by saying this is not a reference to an illness of the mind by which some have medical matters that exist. This is to speak to those who have **elected** an unstable mind through life choices and rejection of the truth in Christ Jesus. The person who has chosen thoughts and actions against the ways of God in other words. Be not mistaken those that do this are mentally unstable for their soul is without the correct guide. The very basic foundational things of the world are very challenging for them to receive. Forever seeking a form of understanding outside of the foundational truths God has instilled. This explains why you see so much confusion being pushed onto the world concerning gender and sex. Words are now created to support the senseless and irrational. Within the church even you see so many false gospels and teachings presented in the pulpit from mentally unstable men and women. You see so many violent crimes in the world from angry, depressed, and confused young people. The mind has so many options it can choose from in this world, which explains what Christ meant by broad is the way to destruction. When you are mentally unstable the very truth enrages you. You see falsehoods as truth and the truth as destructive. You perceive evil as good and good as evil. This was very apparent when Jesus received the ultimate rejection. He was told that his miracles were done from power given by demons. **This showed that people can have such a debased mind that when the very presence of God is right in their face, they cannot even comprehend it as Holy**. Let that sink in for a moment. Notice what Jesus says about such people in John 5:43 **I have come in My Father's name, and you do not receive Me, if another comes in his own name, you will receive him.**

I do not have to provide examples of mankind receiving others that come in their own name. It is a basic function of our society at this point. Many will even receive others that come in their own name that display open wickedness. How else can I describe such people other than mentally unstable. Until the mind and body are one for God you cannot see heaven. These were the words of the Messiah. This is not up for debate as it is written and spoken by Jesus. Renew your mind on the word daily! Let us not think we are immune to mental unstableness without it. Dwell upon all things that are pure and Holy. These things align with Jesus the Christ. Our mind will dwell on being a Holy child of the Father and that will never dissolve, and our mind will be stabilized on truth. Then your earthly life will have the truth of life. Let the mind drink from this. If you choose to, you will find every treasure intended to be kept from you by those who do not desire it. The sound mind needs sound doctrine. Mute minds need nothing but to be controlled by man. For they know not the sound of Christ's voice or words when they hear it. For they are not his.

My deceived experiences

My children, your earthly Dad once struggled with mental stability as it pertained to these topics. Having the word yet not the love of Christ in my life. Having the desire to do what is right, but not the urgency to act upon it. Having the passion for the word and not the wisdom to apply it. My friends, my children, my family. **Please understand this is not of God.** He does not desire you to think on what is righteous alone, he desires you to carry it out just as his son did. **Many truly believe that because they can think about doing the right things, that God is pleased regardless the application of it**. The lie that plagues many is this. The idea that if I can think about the right thing, it proves I have a good heart. So usually, people follow up such thinking with God knows my heart after they display an action opposite of their self-proclaimed thought of righteousness. I once did the same as it comforted me to think I knew God regardless of how I lived. All I was proving when I did this was that I had the information from God to do right. Yet I also proved by not displaying the information with action that I didn't truly believe in God's word, which proved I didn't truly know him. Even worse this deception was comforted with the often misused truth of "Christ died for my sins". This is a very dangerous way of thinking with the context of habitual sin after claiming to follow him. **What else could they mean by this, other than Christ died for me <u>to</u> sin.** This is the thinking of a mentally unstable person that is consumed by fear and exists without knowledge of their true purpose or identity. Usually, entertainment or worldly desire consumes them. **This is the mind that needs to be rejected for love of the world reflects a lack of love for the father.**

Please read what was written in **Hebrews 10:26**.
Dear friends, if we deliberately continue sinning after
we have received the knowledge of the truth, there is
no longer any sacrifice that will cover these sins.
Please understand what this is saying. It is clearly
saying that the mentality of thinking you are covered
to keep sinning after you have been made aware of
the truth is a false thought not from God. If you have
the alertness and the ability to recognize your
thoughts are either of God and not of God, how can
you keep doing what is not of God and claim to love
him. **You are making your choice with better
clarity than a non-believer. There is no sacrifice to
cover that.** You have chosen to walk in what is not of
God with the awareness of his truth. This is
challenging to many I'm sure, but I wonder why it is
easier to believe God is open to you continuing in sin
now, after giving his son who died for it. How does

263

this not expose our hearts in every way by thinking this, and not taking any caution or fear of what we are saying and doing? **This shows a person without righteous self-control.** One that lives with a double mind. The word of God says that such a person is unstable in all their ways and should never think of God to give them anything.

I have lived this false version of Christianity and can tell you it is vain and is manipulatory of others. Desiring to even manipulate God for the sake of living how you want. As it is written the gentiles blaspheme the name of God because of you! There will never be a soothing of the conscience through this self-created belief that is not found in the word of God. Therefore, you find so many claiming to follow Christ angry, depressed, bitter, resentful, and existing with no faith. They believed the lie. The lie that this faith was about getting you to enjoy your worldly desires. The lie that you have no accountability anymore because of what was done for you through Christ Jesus. The lie that if I'm saved, "I'm saved" from consequences of actions I **continue** to make. Consider this. If a man is married to his wife and he claims he is living right with her and that he follows Christ, there are certain behaviors he cannot exhibit. If he does exhibit behaviors such as lying to her and beating her, he consequently is saying those behaviors are him living right and what produces a life in Christ. This form of thinking is what many try to sell as Christianity. Hear my words and disregard my actions. If you try to claim the faith without works you simply expose your faith as dead! **Read James 2:26.** This shows many believe Christ is their alibi for sins instead of the purpose and power for not sinning. This has resulted in lives not aligning

265

with the word of God and even being disregarded as a **necessity**.

Choose today whom to serve

You must **choose** life spiritually in this flesh first! When your body passes away, the invisible is what's left. **The only thing we know in our bodies to be invisible is oxygen and thoughts.** Yet oxygen is a life source, and our thoughts are visualized from within. So, though they appear without visual appearance they are very much real. When oxygen leaves the body, all that is left are our thoughts. This means that it is what goes to the eternal realm where the ultimate life source is. Either those thoughts are with The Father in Heaven through his son Jesus Christ or to the realm that does not receive his sons' teachings'. Remember this! **This is the message I**

have for you. Think of your choices (decisions) as guaranteed memories that will stand before God. **If you do not see the choice in life as a memory you wish to carry with you to God the Father, turn from it immediately!!** This is for those that already claim to be in the Lord. For those who have yet to come to the Lord, understand he is desiring to wipe your past clean and give you a new life in him. I urge you to heed my words. You see everyone thinks of feeling "good" for the moment. It would be safe to say if it were up to our flesh every single decision would be based on that desire. You are not a prisoner nor a slave to this flesh any-longer if you believe in Jesus. So, think first about your purpose in Christ. Submit to what is appropriate for your mind, and your soul according to the word of God. When you renew your mind with God's word, you find that your decisions are more thoughtful and considerate of Christ. Intern, they become more thoughtful and considerate of others. Notice the pattern? Your selfishness is not being considered here as the priority, for you are no longer living for you. Your life is in Christ, so trust that he knows what's best for you. Furthermore, you don't have to listen to someone tell you what's best for you or seek it for yourself because a major part of following Christ comes with the requirement of **first denying yourself.** Your mind is either for you or against you. You oversee your mind so whom you submit it to shows whom you trust. Train it, stabilize it or it will consume and control you. Many have lived thinking they were wise or more righteous than another. Yet all that have lived since the beginning of the world have found none of us are different outside of Christ. We all deal with the same things. We all have flesh that will die. In Christ we all are the same as well in the fact that we shall live eternally with him so don't let pride poison your mind. Trust what God says above everyone else's mentality or what the world says is good. Don't find yourself deceived by anyone, especially not the one closest to you. The one closest to you and your own way of thinking is **you.**

Shalom (Peace)

שְׁבִיעִי (shvi'i)

<u>The Riches of Humility</u>

This word humility is a word that comes with so many layers. It's impossible to detail all of them. The main reason is that its power comes without it being spoken. It's true- identity is found without the effort of trying. The one with it doesn't intend to show it for any vain reason but displays it as if it has attached itself to them without their knowledge. This person would never say they are humble because again true humility isn't found in pride or boasting. Without the Holy Spirit no-one can produce this fruit of the spirit truly with the right heart. **I simply seek to speak on why it is impossible to obtain if you are of the world.**

The main reason a person has love of the world in them is because the love of the Father is not truly desired by them. Read **1 John 2:15**. A critical way we find that we are without humility is if we believe we are above **reproach.** Meaning our ways should not be questioned as if they are the ways of God completely. No-one is above reproach! Now the obvious exception to this will always be a person upholding the word of God. Anyone that questions those ways are not questioning you but rather God himself. With that said, if you read the book of Job, you will see questioning God gets a person nowhere, but in a position to be humbled ironically. Those who exalt themselves will be humbled by God and that is not what anyone should want. **Seriously! It is a terrible and fearful thing to fall into the hands of the living God.**

Stay away from the false prophets

It is written to not believe every spirit, for every spirit is not from God. As it is written in **1 John 4:1**, many false prophets have gone out into the world. We have been as sheep amongst wolves. This is a spiritually literal statement made in the word of God. In case you have never seen wolves attack sheep, I tell you the image is brutal. Sometimes I feel that image should be on our minds when considering what men or women we listen to concerning the word of God.

Be careful of the one in this world who clothes himself in white garments and is called by his followers Holy Father. You have but one Holy Father and He is in Heaven. You are to call no-one Father but Him as it is spoken by the Messiah in **Matthew 23:9-11**. All the days of your life are to be taken one at a time. No one has lived now or before you that could promise another day to themselves. So, don't give regard to such men that wish to be glorified here on earth as Holy. There is only one that is good and that is The Heavenly Father as stated by our Lord in **Mark 10:18.** With that said, no one has ever given birth to themselves. Not one. God did this to show us his infinite power and grace. This was done to remind us to be humble while in this flesh. We all needed a mom and dad for this flesh to begin forming and then nurtured. So, we needed someone from our very beginning. If your time on earth is lived with the understanding of the Father's grace, mercy, and most important Love for you. **You will be rich beyond measure**. Simply put, you need the Lord God through **Yeshua the Anointed to form you and nurture you spiritually**. No-one is here to be called your teacher but Jesus Christ. He is your teacher. Anyone claiming to be such is in error. For we are all brothers and sisters in him. **Read Matthew 23:8-10**. There is no teaching that can be given but what was already provided. They are to simply read what was written while assisting their brothers and sisters with better understanding if they have been given that gift. **Be careful of these men that wish to create humorous sermons, and creative doctrines on life to tickle your ears.** These sorts of errors by them lead many to destruction. Valuing the possessions of the world above the spiritual knowledge they have been called to bring to their flock. That flock is God's flock first. Not theirs. Do not be intimidated and afraid to examine them and their teachings. Love them enough to confront them if you find them in error with gentle confrontation and knowledge to support zeal.

Test their spirit with the scriptures in peace and love. Do not be as some are towards them. Hostile and angry. You are not called to such behavior. Your savior already addressed them with his Godly zeal. They have already been judged. Prove your understanding of his words by following his commandments. That is to love. So correct and reprove in love. Though you may be given discernment against their ways they are still your brother and sister in the faith. They may not be willfully deceiving others and may value your correction. You may gain a true brother or sister in the faith because of this. Christ and his angels will separate the wheat from the tares. We are not called to do that as it is written for some wheat would be uprooted as well. Let God have his final judgements. Let us correct in love in hopes to not lose a brother or sister to the lake of fire. If such a person does not receive your correction or efforts to remove such ways that are not of God, you ought to remove yourself from their presence as to not taint yourself with hypocrisy.

Reject your fleshly desires

There are many things that desire to cling to our flesh. The most common finds itself within our words. Let us set aside foolish talk as it adds nothing to us. See it as a subtraction from you that you cannot afford. Let the wise man show his wisdom in how he lives as written in **James 3:13.** Rise in this flesh! Overcome the things that come naturally to you! You will meet humility if you do so. The lustful desires, the foolish thoughts, the need for meaningless downtime. This is much of what the flesh's life consumes itself of. Let the peace of Christ be your peace. Let your no be your no to people and your yes be your yes. Don't be double minded in your words and actions. Even the world frowns upon that sort of behavior. Be graceful and merciful to those who may be seen as lesser to you. Who are you to perceive someone as inferior? What manner of living are you able to take with you after death that they don't have? Quickly, answer this! What man-made possession was guaranteed to you in the afterlife? Not even one! So, think not much of yourself and the things you have. Don't let that be your measuring stick on a person's value. The same air you breathe was exhaled by that same person. For God gave it to you both just as he gave to the trees and the animals. Every flesh desire is uncontrollable if welcomed. When it comes to **appetite, anger, or sexual attraction** the flesh will consume you into a bottomless pit once you submit to it. Be on guard against these. They are disregarded by the world as common to your flesh and encouraged to be indulged in as necessary dependent on the circumstance. This is the justification for each that plagues many. **Now each is encouraged to be received as a positive identity in this generation.** Now the glutton with an attitude is celebrated. The perverse and lustful are decorated as peaceful and loving. This generation gloats about what must be rejected. My children, be wise to this and think not yourselves strong enough on your own to resist. We all **NEED** the Holy Spirit and the grace of God to resist such ways of indulgence.

Be careful how you treat others

Many have treated angels with hospitality without knowing it, and many have harshly. As written in **Hebrews 13:2**. Be careful how you entreat strangers. God forbid we treat one harshly simply because of the perception of that individual as a lowly person. Christ spoke to this by simply saying how you treated that person is how you treated me as it is written in **Matthew 25:45**. **Remember this!** Treat your enemies with love and compassion. This is foolishness to the world, but the word of God says let the one who thinks he is wise, become a fool so that he may become truly wise as written in **1 Corinthians 3:18-20**. Mans' knowledge and deep thoughts are foolishness to God. So, when you perceive a person as less than you, you are full of yourself and exist with a feeble mind.

There are basic foundations of truth that are required so that any form of humility can exist. To start, let's speak about treating your mom and dad with respect and honor. This creates the foundation of your understanding. How can you honor God and disrespect your parents? Without them, your flesh wouldn't exist. **If you cannot respect those that created your flesh, how be it possible to respect the one that created your soul?** Stand on the word of God. To those that question why you are so different, simply say I'm here to serve my Father in Heaven. If that offends anyone and it will, let their offence be their stumbling block not yours. Doing what is right will always remain a requirement, let your confirmation be that God will reward you. As it is written in **Luke 6:22**, you are blessed when people speak harshly towards you or choose to not associate with you for Christ's sake. **You are blessed because**

of these things. Your flesh will attempt to stir up a desire to avoid these things. If you walk in Christ, this is **unavoidable.** God does not give the spirit of fear but of **power, love, and self-discipline.** These things are your armor against such attacks. I tell you this so that you may welcome humility in doing this in response to the ways of the world. I tell you the truth. **How you treat others, reflects how you view God and how much love you have for Christ, or the lack thereof.** To the one who can understand this, apply it!

There are many that are remembering daily the faults of another. Even their very own parents. Feeling completely justified because of the wrongs that have been committed towards them. This form of vision will always blind you toward actions that cannot be seen clearly. Bitterness, revenge, rage, jealousy, envy, and disrespect have all led to the most heinous crimes ever committed. You would think those crimes were only committed towards the people that the criminal had these blind emotions towards directly. What you will find is that those that did not do wrong to these criminals were affected also. The very people that felt wronged by another went on to wrong others. Deeply disturbing actions done to people who have never met them or ever wronged them. Therefore, the blind emotions of such fleshly ways are intended by the evil one to be passed down or affect whomever you come close to. It is a self-imposed disease of the mind to treat others wrongly. It is blinded by the foundational sin from the beginning which is **selfishness.** Self-centered vision blinds us to others. It is the ultimate disregard for any living creature or being. The Messiah spoke to this with an alarming revelation in **Matthew 6:22-23**. He states [22] "The eye is the lamp of the body; so then, if your eye is clear, your whole body will be full of light. ²³ But if your eye is bad, your whole body will be full of darkness. So, if the light that is in you is darkness, how great is the darkness! Talk about a mic drop moment. Don't deceive yourself. Self-centered vision is darkness, and you cannot see truly yourself or others through that lens.

Your faith must have Christ vision

Some translations for this scripture use the word **single**, for if your eye is single your whole body will be full of light. **Here is the point, if you cannot see the single most important thing for your life, you do not see clearly. In fact, your entire body will be full of darkness and great is that darkness for it will direct every interaction you have.** As it pertains to faith in Christ, please know it is not blind. It gives you true sight. It is what gives you the vision to see the purpose of your existence. Without it, you cannot see clearly. Oh, trust me, the evil one from within knows how to deceive you into believing that the way you see is just fine. **I have been there.** Claiming to know God because I can articulate topics in the bible or speak with great conviction that the world is evil. I could debate and present sound reasons for the existence of God. No-one could tell me I didn't know God. My apologetics were sound and precise. Yet my faith was without action so even the light I had was darkness for it was not directed by love. It lacked humility on depths to this day I'm confounded by. All I know is that the very road to hell is broad and it is paved with the deception of right intent. **The greatest deception among all is the idea that we know God.** This is the blind faith that has so much pride and arrogance within it that it is truly the hardest to be removed. We see this clearly during the time of Jesus's life on earth. The ones with the hardest of hearts, the ones that challenged his teachings and miracles above all were those that thought they knew God. I can only present this notion to you. What if instead of thinking you know God, you examine your life and let him show you what areas reflect the opposite. Then a profound thing will take place. The one with a true desire for all their heart to be given to God will speak that they do not know him. Once this comes to the surface, the one true living God will show up to reveal himself to you. This is because God is near the humble. The challenge I present to everyone is the revelation God has given me. **Ask yourself, does your life really know Jesus?** Are you willing to be searched by his Holy Spirit so it can be revealed to you? Or do you prefer the level of knowledge you claim to have already of him? Every single one of us can sit and ponder these questions. Instead, the questions amongst this generation continue to be the product of not knowing God. So, questions are asked like what is the purpose of life? Now we have a generation that has progressed to full rebellion and ask questions like if God is truly good why does he let bad things happen? These questions reveal the lack of knowing God. Those in rebellion towards God ask questions without desire for answers for no answer would suffice. As for the church, those questions have started to creep in also and even greater questions have come forth that challenge God on his word as truth. This is astounding, for we once thought the questions of open non-believers were disrespectful. Yet what can compare to this mockery of the faith from those who claim it? Even so, we have the more seasoned believers that still ask questions like these. What do you have for me to do in this life

God? What is my purpose God? All these questions assume we know God. **If we knew him, we would see the answers within his written words.** The truth is many have read his words concerning these questions, the answers are just not sufficient for them. As the answer is to walk in **true life.** To live the life on the teachings of Christ. What God has for you is salvation through this! So often we see this treated as some minor consolation prize. The immediate thought is what about life on earth. How am I to enjoy living here until you bring me home? So many questions that show our thoughts are still captivated by our love for the world. It is not enough to live a righteous life; it is not enough to love others and let the light of God be reflected through such. Many are not fulfilled by the life of following Christ. Yet this is to be enough for us. Truth is, it isn't for many, yet a belief one can know God with that mind still is received by such claiming the faith. We feel our faith sees correctly. Yes, our faith should have sight indeed. The question is, what is your faith trying to truly see? Does your faith care if it is correctly seeing God?

We understand already that this flesh life ends in death. So, for those that are content with that, they shall reap what they sowed into it. The Father is just in all his ways. He would prefer that no-one might perish. It is not to his delight that any should see eternal damnation. Yet it is to the desire of mankind that boasts in its pride that ignores or forgets its fate. With that, each person chooses its end. Some with a contention that alarms the very earth itself. Be not found with those that carelessly disregard the truth. Also, be not partakers of those that recklessly deceive themselves by claiming the faith with their mouth and not with their hearts. For God judges the heart.

Anyone that chooses to neglect their responsibilities in Christ for gain and acknowledgment is choosing to be judged by God. This is because they believe that if the world doesn't know their true self, they can get away with whatever they choose. This is foolish for God knows the depths of every heart. The true wickedness of every imagination. Nothing escapes him. So be not blind to this. Faith in Christ brings attention to these areas. It is the light that exposes the darkness of one's true self. Truth is we all have faith in something or someone, for our way of living reflects such. The question is simply this; Is your faith truly in Christ alone? If it is not, your faith cannot see the truth. **The truth about yourself.**

Seek a heart after God

Without the right heart, you cannot love another let alone God. There are a lot of damaged people with bitterness in their hearts claiming to know love and claiming to know God. In the world you see the word love is used and abused daily. I cannot think of another word that gets misused and misrepresented daily than this. Be not deceived many are using this word in place of the words they mean to say such as **"I need you"**; or **"I idolize you"**. In this generation that's what people usually mean when they say I love you to others. Once the love of God is in you, your whole understanding of what love is; gets changed. You find that your love doesn't require feedback to be still true and genuine. It doesn't idolize the person as idolatry is not of God. It doesn't need anything from that person for your love to stay pure and true. **This is the love of God.** For **while** we were in sin, he sent his son as a sacrifice to redeem us. There was no love shown to God that prompted his decision to save us. We showed him no love. There were great sins done against him constantly and still are. Yet it is his love and his goodness that are questioned. You truly cannot make this stuff up. With that, he sends his mercy and his grace every single day. We are to receive this truth and recognize his love as a love that our natural flesh selves have no comprehension of. **For surely, we would never consider giving a loved one's life for an enemy to live**. Regardless of what anyone believes, humanity knows the truth of this matter. Even if you hated your family, you would never let them die so the stranger that hates you could live. Let that humble our perspectives with sorrow and revelation of who we are compared to God. Having said this, understand God does not desire to save his enemy. He desires to change the one whom lived like his enemy into the very righteous soul that will dwell with him forever. We clearly need his son and his spirit to have a heart to even be respectful towards God. I cannot imagine anything more needed for this generation. **New hearts!** People will stand in long lines for the latest tennis shoes, cell phone, television, and sale event. Packing the doorways for just a glimpse of these like they do on Black Fridays! As for a new heart, most cannot tolerate a 30 second conversation concerning it. Yes, a new heart should be sought after with even greater diligence as our very soul depends on it. I cannot stress this enough as it is the truth. The truth must be received, for there is no other way to be set free.

KNOW THE TRUTH AND BE SET FREE

שְׁמִינִ֖י (shmini)

<u>Pre-sent Revelation</u>

Living through the prophetic judgements in the

book of revelation

I shall address what is already unfolding before our

very eyes. This is what I see and what has already

been written in the word of God. Living during these

times I have witnessed the birth of evil that masks

itself as good. This is the foundation of what the end

will consist of. However long God allows this no one

knows, but the plan has been put in place by the powers of this world. Thinking they are doing something against God's plan but in fact, simply following the prophesied end already written by John. They cannot see it, thus fulfilling **Corinthians 1:19** as true when it says he chose the foolish things of the world to shame the wise. The folly of mankind has become so regarded by the people it has been given a voice and power as the world's truth. That folly with a voice that's been given power will ultimately bring forth its own demise. With that said, the coming fall of this world is inevitable. **It has already begun.** Instead of trying to turn from its ways, it believes God will bless it because of the creative false love it stands by. Having no awareness of its pending destruction already taking place they continue in deceitfulness. Wildfires, hurricanes, famines, and extreme heat coupled with diseases are simply the seals being opened as it is written in the book of revelation. This shall spread throughout the world continuously and escalate to new heights. There is no future without these things. We see that we have become accustomed to these things as normal. Even more, we see violence and rebellion as another social norm when it takes place. This shows we are headed towards the end. Completely living amongst the birth pains.

Living amongst the Birth Pains

In my opinion, every seal written in the book of revelation to be opened has but **two!** Let that sink in for a minute. The 6th and 7th seal is what awaits this generation. **We are living during the 4th and 5th seals.** As the 4th seal was opened, we have witnessed in the 20th century more deaths than any other. The 4th seal is written to be various forms of death. Death from violence, famine, diseases, and killings by wild beasts. Yes, that time of death was so normal that it was videotaped as evidence for all to see. Some even watch such things for entertainment. Gross darkness across the land. It's portrayed by those in power and maintained by those in poverty. It's used as a tool to control the masses with fear and diversion. In other lands, we see diseases and famines as the norm. With the recent pandemic of 2020, the world has shifted into a new understanding of its times. This should be an understanding that these things happening are not just happening in remote lands but rather are here to affect all. Even a non-believer can see things are off in the world. This has been taking place for hundreds of years. Meaning the times have been upon us. This pandemic was just this generation's turn to experience it. The **5th seal** has its structure under way. The sad truth is that living in this country we are blinded so often by what is happening in others. The persecution of Christians in the eastern parts of the world is astounding. The beheading of believers and the destruction of church buildings are the norm there. So, when you see so little coverage of it from a media that loves to exploit the "**oppression**" of people. You know it's not by accident. Those in control of what you see intentionally don't want you to see it or hear about it. Now this **5th seal** is described as a great persecution during the reign from the man of perdition. Those who will reject him and refuse to follow his structure will be persecuted. Currently in the west, true Christians are persecuted through lies and manipulation. Called hate speakers when scripture is read that speaks out against the sinful lifestyles paraded around in this world as love or rights. So, you see the foundation is being laid so when this persecution comes from the Anti-Christ the people will not recognize it as such but will welcome it for the betterment of their society.

The 21st century is upon us. We are 20 plus years into it, and no one can deny with the recent war in Israel everyone is on high alert of the times. College students protest their views and opinions of that war, and the church proclaims its views from the word of God about it all. The time to open your eyes has been upon us as the man of perdition is being prepared to make his appearance in this century! You must understand these events are structured and calculated. A major focus on what needs to be in place prior to the evil appearing is the urbanization of all the continents. For everyone to follow a structure, everyone must be living more closely together. This is happening on every continent and will continue until those that are putting this in place are satisfied. Satisfied that all people are close enough economically and socially for the instructions to be easily implemented. Those instructions will alter the way everyone is identified. The easiest way to do so is to utilize the technology and come up with an electronic identification system that can be input into the human. Something that is easily scanned by law enforcement and throughout the world collectively. The assets and funds one will have will only be accessed through this device at grocery stores, airports and anywhere you can purchase items. There will be no way to live without this device implanted in your hand or forehead. Those in Christ living during the time of this will be given the discernment to know what this is. They will be laughed at and considered crazy for what they say about this during that time. Mainly because it will be on the heels of another catastrophic event. This will ensure the mark is received amongst fear. It will even be presented as an necessity for safety even. Fear is the tool of the evil one. This will be presented as a safe way to live once it is rolled out. Christians that stand with the word of God will continue to be seen as those that stir conflict with the way others wish to live. Yet it is the word of God that conflicts with their lives. **So, we are hated for the word's sake**. Praise the Most High in Christ!! Read **Matthew 5:11-12**. What better reason to be hated? This means our father loves us for we are blessed when men shall revile us and persecute us. When they speak all manner of evil falsely against us for Christ's sake, we are blessed indeed. For we love him regardless of the consequences presented to us. We know he is with us. For we speak the truth and do not accept the corruption and open wickedness the world desires to make normal. This is the church pronouncing its rightful judgement on earth. For we were told that what we bound on earth shall be bound in heaven. The true followers of Christ cannot accept the lies and deception pushed upon others. Gods' kingdom is to be on earth as it is in heaven. So, we are to treat our lives as such. We are to love others with the truth for it is how we are loved. Satan desires we shut up, and let people perish deceived. Many of those people have believed the lie in this country that if it makes you happy to live against Gods' way, then it is your life to indulge. The lie is that those who agree with your open sin, love you. Furthermore, those who speak against it hate you. This is the deception that has been normalized here in America and abroad. There are many that are fighting to stand against this movement of sin. In this country not all are on board with the destruction of family and the killing of infants, not all are on board with same sex lifestyles or trans ideology being imposed on children. It is not the country to blame but rather everyone that stands for such open evil while calling it good. This shall be judged. This sin will not be forgiven on earth or in heaven.

The future of America

As for this country, I cannot speak to another. The ways of God and his word is not respected here by the masses. The internal disconnect from God will result in a disfunction that no land has ever recovered from. Rather its structure becomes desolate. Typically, a country has a position on social and economic standards it wishes to uphold. Here in this country, there appears to be a power which operates in accordance with its own demise. I point this out because you must not follow this regime. You must not look to the world for answers. This applies to every nation on this planet. If I'm telling you to depart from the world it is because this world hates Christ. The direction it is heading in is one that will appear to seek peace, love, and unity from all people. **Rather none of those will be through Christ.** If you do not know God's truth, love and peace, the world will appear appealing to you. You will seek to be unified with the regime presenting their version. This will result in you being deceived by the power structure of the world as they present their version to you. At some point, the world will exhaust all efforts for this and give its overall power to the one that sits on earth dressed in white claiming to be Holy. Those in power must get to a place where they are not capable of fulfilling the plan of unity. So, they call him Holy Father and he presents himself as God on earth for them. **Do not follow or listen to this man.** He is a false prophet and is not of God. Let the one with wisdom understand. We already see how those that preach in the streets are treated. Those that do this are seen as criminals pushing hate speech today and will be persecuted more in the future. This will become law and the actual words in the Holy Bible will be banned worldwide or changed to suit the evil in the world. Violence shall become the norm towards the men and woman who stand against the efforts to legalize such decisions. Imprisonment will be normalized as there will be a law that eventually addresses speaking the gospel in public in America. Disturbing the peace is the charge of today but soon it will be more extreme. Citing hate speech, or claiming they are **anti-peacemakers.** The **true** Christian will be mocked and ridiculed by the interfaith regime with made up words that deem the truth violent. This will be the persecution of the church in America. Those that are conservative must guard themselves against the deception that these laws are to promote peace. They will be caught off guard because of the natural disasters that will begin to cause major chaos in this country and the world. That will be the shaking done by God. Those who love the world and the things within it will cling to the desire for normalcy. In doing such they will accept laws and ways of living apart from God. The pride of the world will be on full display as the Lord begins sending more strong delusions to those rebelling against him. The depths of evil and wickedness many will be involved in will feel like a movie, as many people will be open pagans or part of Satanic cults. This will be the culture glorified and promoted to children as where peace and love is.

Christ separates you

Christ said he came to divide not bring peace; he wanted to divide you from the world not bring you into peace with their ways. Read **Matthew 10:34-36.** Living in peace with everyone we should do, but not at the expense of receiving their sinful ways into our lives or openly agreeing with sin. This is the deception of the devil. That deception is that you cannot truly love a person without receiving their sinful ways or agreeing with it for the sake of peace. God desires us to be the light to this world. How can we be the light agreeing with darkness? Do you see darkness trying to agree with the light? Let the one with wisdom understand. Read **John 3:19.** This world has already been judged because it has rejected the light when it was sent here. Not because the light didn't bring the truth or because there is some other truth but because men loved their evil deeds more. So essentially, they preferred darkness, or being separated from God. Consider that truly for a second. The world prefers the perverse and lustful things, the rationale that justifies lying and having hatred. It desires to glorify pride in these things. It rather the spirit of fear over the Spirit of truth. It loves coveting and disrespecting others, even their parents. The world loves the idolization of people, possessions, and lofty dreams to aspire for materialism and status. It loves its own self-proclaimed wisdom as it pertains to deep thoughts above the word of God. We see in our time the fight for rights above morality. So, the world despises what is morally right if it confronts the comfort of life. Even if that means terminating the life **you** created in your own womb. The evil of these times uses the horrible events that have happened to others to justify their desires to carry out wickedness. So, a person that truly hates taking responsibility for their actions tries to justify terminating their child by speaking on victims of rape or incest that results in a pregnancy. Do you see the depth of cruelty here? Instead of taking responsibility for the actions one has committed, the mind in the world will try to excuse it by using the hardships of others that do not pertain to oneself. If my justification to commit evil comes from the fact that evil was done to me, how can I claim the one that treated me evil to be wrong? Can a man that was molested as a child use that experience to excuse his actions or desires to do such to a child when he becomes an adult? Of course not!! This is the Satanic mind in the world. The often-stated "necessary evil" perception. Those who desire to think like this will find themselves alongside the very same people that support children altering their bodies to change genders. Those same people love to parade the streets with lustful driven attire claiming love of all things. There is no secret that these are all linked together as a stance on **choice and rights**. This generation is fighting for the acceptance to carry out the evil in their hearts. **Our Lord does not want you to be at peace with these lies or in support of them**. Receive the hardships and the name calling! This is nothing compared to the wrath and judgement of God that is surely to come! I share this with you so that you might know anyone aligning themselves with such people will receive the same punishment and judgement. If you are claiming Christ and aligning with such people, you are an enemy of God. For because of you the heathen blasphemes his name. It is better if you had never heard the word of God. Take this very seriously for in case you have not noticed, God has allowed this generation to grow in its way of thinking to reveal those who truly are of him and those who claim him in vain. If you cannot handle the ridicule that comes along withstanding on the truth concerning sexual immorality, then you are not fit for the Kingdom of God. For this is the least hidden sin amongst us that openly rejects what God has to say about it. Christ Jesus was clear in **Matthew 10:34 when he said, "think not that I came to bring peace to the world". No, but a sword.** That a man would be in opposition to his very own household concerning the truth. Now if this is the case concerning your own household what manner of thinking considers those outside of it as it pertains to the truth in Christ. Jesus is being clear here. He came to separate you from the world as it concerns the truth of the one true God and Father. As the days draw near it is time to see that God is preparing his church for its coming persecution as a whole.

Fear of offending leads to destruction

Remember this. You can love people without agreeing with their ways. When God says to be a friend of the world is to be his enemy. **That's what he means.** If you are a friend to the sinful lifestyles people live in rejection of God, meaning you excuse them or even state they aren't sins so that you may not offend. Let me state it again. **You are his enemy.** The message of the world is that true love must agree with or respect the ways of others for the sake of peace. That the sinful lifestyles listed in the word of God are not sin just because this "so called" outdated book says so. Well, the Bible also says not to lie, kill, or steal. Yet no one fights against those things to prove them as good to do. Yet if you listen close enough you will hear things such as, "well I only told a little white lie", or "I should have the right to terminate my pregnancy" and "it was only this small item I took from work". You see this generation does reject all of

God's ways. **It has more justifications to do the things God says not to do than any justification to obey him.** Many rather not offend the person doing these things. It's because many have the same thoughts and understand the impulses. It's as if they respect the boldness of those that act them out. So, to make ourselves feel better about our sinful thinking we created justifications for all sin. For all can relate to sin. The desire to be relatable in this area creates cowardice within us. Instead of relating to God we have preferred to relate to the sinful nature of others because we have a past or current that mirrors them. What a paralyzing and sorrowful existence to fear man more than God. To fear man to the degree that God himself is disregarded because you have more in common with sin shows a lack of love for God. Great power has been given to willful sinning people because of the fear to offend, and its root comes from

313

the lack of identity we have in Christ. What is missed so often is when we claim to love someone by excusing sin, we are showing a lack of love towards them by not telling them the truth. We also show a lack of knowledge concerning who Christ is and a lack of belief in the power of the Holy Spirit. The old saying goes, you can put makeup and lipstick and a dress on a pig, but it will still be a pig. This generation is upset that some will never call that pig anything but a pig. You cannot make this up. Clearly strong delusions have been sent by God as prophesied in **2 Thessalonians 2:11.** Consider that this is just the beginning of strong delusions. Read **2 Timothy 3:13,** it says evil men and seducers will get worse and worse. Prepare yourself to see even greater wickedness as the days draw near the end.

A generation of proud hypocrites

The hypocrisy of this world is astounding. Here are those hypocrisies.

It is said that no one should impose their rights upon another, unless it is the rights of women concerning their unborn child. Then the child's rights shouldn't infringe upon the mother, but the mother can infringe upon the right of the child. That right is the right to life. Furthermore, women should not be called women anymore but rather "birthing persons" to not infringe on the rights of a man who now identifies as a trans woman. That man has the right to infringe upon those who identify as woman from birth as it pertains to their sports and activities and restrooms.

A homosexual lifestyle is justified and glorified, as love is love. Seeing as though loving a friend of the same sex platonically isn't the desire or what's being disputed. They expose what their slogan truly means.

As it reads with deceit for it means to say "Sex is Sex". Which by that logic means you cannot love a person without having sexual relations with them.

Here is another, children should have the right to live as the gender of their choice. Yet it is with the guidance of their parents to do so. For it is the parents that facilitate the drugs and surgeries for the child. I tell you the truth, if human flesh had not lived to see these logics being lived out, we would never have considered such a time as this. These are the logics existing in the world right now. How can anyone not see that God has sent a strong delusion upon this world. We are afraid to not offend any of these topics because the enemy has done a creative job in our imaginations to understand these very destructive ways of existence. Calling our fear and lack of love for others compassion. These ways of existing bring no life to the person nor anyone else. **All these ways of living are designed to end life fleshly and spiritually**. The wicked powers and spirits in high places that are behind all of this know very well this is about the death of humanity and this is the evil one's plan to bring it forth. The hypocrisy of it all is that every human being has benefited from a heterosexual relationship that did not abort them. To even fight for the right to engage in these ways requires a complete rejection of what brought you forth. Even more it rejects the very one that created that nature of being to do so. That is the one true living God. **All this fighting to have the right to end life and enjoy relationships that cannot create any. Where there is hypocrisy there you will find Satan.**

Many people are listening to these lies on how this frees a person or how it brings joy and happiness to their life to live in these ways. **Neglecting the fact that children are being attacked here**. If it is not killing them in the womb, it's informing them that their existence can be false and needs altering. Somehow a child should be responsible enough to make those decisions when we have a consensus of neuroscientists that agree, the brain development specifically the cerebral cortex that controls thinking, and decision making doesn't fully develop until the mid-'to late 20s for us as humans. So, if you reject the scientific studies from neuroscientists, what information are you using to evaluate a child making these choices? People aren't using any understanding, not biblical world views nor scientific ones. This is truly a new era of thinking that people are using, and it doesn't have any basis of truth, just desire. There has never been a time where this much information is available to a person. To reject so much information shows a rebellion on levels the world has never seen. The rejection of God in the wilderness by the Hebrews he led out of slavery was done out of fear and ignorance. Fear is being used as well by this generation but more by those who know better, and ignorance is displayed by those who do not. Most people who are pro-choice, are pro-homosexual and pro-transgender lifestyles as well. The common thread with them all is the cutoff of creation. **So, the same person that would be fine with that child dead, is now speaking on what choices that child should be able to make about their gender.** Truth is under attack and that attack has taken place here in these times. I recall a host on a popular tv show speak blasphemy against Christ. Her statement was that Jesus would be leading the LGBTQ parades if he were on earth today. This would never be uttered about Mohammed concerning the Muslim faith that condemns such lifestyles also. Did you catch that? There is a strategic intention to ensure the world views Jesus as everything they want him to be rather than who he is. To be very direct and clear he would not support any of this. It is Jesus that tells us it be better the person that causes one of these little ones to stumble or fall, be thrown into a lake with a millstone around their neck. Read **Matthew 18:6.** That sounds like a man that takes the corruption of children very seriously! So, while the debased mind continues to try and create a destructive generation that has such empathy for death and sin, and such enmity with life and correction, God stays the same. God in his judgement will be just towards them. If you have found yourself drifting towards such beliefs, I plead with you to depart from the lie and let God save your soul for those who have encouraged this will receive a stern judgement. Especially if you claim

Christ, for you blaspheme his name in associating him with wickedness. There is no forgiveness for such blasphemy!

Do not fear-Be encouraged

We love in truth and in spirit. This is our worship. A friend of the world is an enemy of God. This will not be the message of the one dressed in white that they call Father. The interfaith movement is an Anti-Christ movement. Trying to convince the world that there are many ways to God is a direct teaching against the truth of Christ who is the way, the truth, and the life. I call it an Anti-Christ movement because its purpose is to inform people of a message **opposite** of what Christ said. **Christ said no-one comes to the Father but through me**. When Christ was tempted, he was informed that if he served Satan, he would be given power over all the kingdoms of the earth. This of course was rejected by Christ but the one dressed in white they call Holy Father here on earth will accept this offer if he hasn't already. The world wishes to bring everyone **together in peace**. On the surface, this doesn't sound bad at all, but you must remember the world hates Christ, so this is being done in rejection of him. To do such a thing, the world must receive all ways and walks of life. Yet the word of God says to stay away from certain walks of life like homosexuality, drunkenness, immorality, idolatry, witchcraft, and things of this nature. If the one claiming to be righteous and of God is excusing even one of these, he is false and is teaching deception. Be not deceived! Do not deceive yourself! Yes, you will be scoffed at, laughed at, ridiculed, and even persecuted. You will be told that God's word teaches hatred. Fear not, God loved us enough to inform us this would happen so we could be prepared in his word with his spirit. The world hates what is truly pure and good. Be what the world hates. For it is what God desires for you. Use the life God has given you to honor him. Your life is **not** your own. You see, the sins, the pride and boasting of this generation are the reasons for the judgement of God as written in **Colossians 3:6**. So be strong in faith and worry not about what is to come for our Heavenly Holy Father knows how to protect his own. He cannot lie so the fact he has promised those in the faith of his son's life eternally means death has no power over us. Remember this when death comes, whether violently or in old age, remember this when jailed and beaten. Let us take joy that we be treated as Jesus was treated for his sake. This is not for the faint of heart. This walk with Christ remains only for those that truly love the one true living God.

Only a pure heart will survive

Understand good works do not please God if done with an impure heart. For God judges the heart. In these times they will celebrate things of perverse nature masking themselves as good. The rights of such perverse things will be fought for. Once those that practice these ways gain power in political forums they will be celebrated even more. This will dismiss the content of character for the content of lifestyle. All the while telling you your lifestyle in Christ is hatred towards them. **The land that does this will fall into arrogance and its' pride will lead to its demise**. You should come out of this land and recognize its ways shall bring even greater judgments to come. Even so, already present. Plagues and conflicts will only increase. Those that claim to be on the right-side hate those that claim to be on the right-side. Both hate each other so whose side are they on? If you have hatred in your heart towards **people,** you are on the **wrong side.** There is no right there. Simply hate what is evil and love what is good. I do not hate any of the people living in these lifestyles depicted or thinking in these ways. It is love that requires me to expose the deception of such living. People truly have no idea of what they do. I know I didn't, and I sinned while claiming to know God. So, I was no better than anyone living fully convinced they are good with God while indulging in desires. I understand they are just consumed by desire and lust, powered by self-centeredness. They know what they want, and they do not care about the truth so when I say they truly have no idea what they do. I mean they have no comprehension of the consequences to come nor the love that was sent to free them. Therefore, the demise of those who reject this information shall be quick.

The land that condoned it all will fall. For God is not mocked, whatsoever a man sows he shall reap, and the land built on wickedness shall crumble and be no more.

Countries from afar will marvel at the fall of the land that has condoned this. For it will be a great fall! If you were wise, you'd leave this land. Leave its ways I should say! Amongst it all, new powers will form and assume themselves the leaders of the world. They are corrupt as well in their ways. As one power leaves, another assumes the role with the same objectives. To control the masses and to do things without Christ. How can we understand this matter? Know this. If they knew God, they would never revere a man here and call him Holy Father. They would never abuse the truth by perverting it for gain. Fear would have overtaken them if they loved God, so much so that every single word out of their mouths would have been carefully examined before uttered in a pulpit. Those that are blind wish to do what they wish to do so the truth eludes them. God has given them over to their heart's desires. With that said, all the books of revelations will continue to be fulfilled as they have already begun. If you find yourself on the end of this wondering if it applies to you, it be better to ask God to examine your heart than to dismiss this. It is better if you examine me and these words than discredit them due to my lack of status. The time is coming, even so it is at hand. For every heart not completely invested purely in Christ shall be exposed.

Revelation 3:10

"Because you have obeyed my command to persevere, I will protect you from the

great time of testing that will come upon the whole world to test those who belong to this world.

I can do nothing of myself

I am fully aware that the world if ever to read this will have many names to call me. Many accusations against me. I have no problem making it clear that I have been the least of men on earth and I do not say that with honor or boasting but rather embarrassment and sorrow. By that I mean, I have done many wrongs to those that have loved me and those that haven't. Through my selfishness, arrogance, pride, lust, sadness, depression, and anxiety I opened myself up to birth lies, fornication, deception, manipulation, and outbursts of anger. Above this, I have been a reprobate in that I was claiming Christ while living this way. I am beyond thankful for the forgiveness God has granted me. I am in awe of his mercy upon my life. His grace upon my existence. Without his Holy Spirit I cannot understand why I was left here to live after living in such a wicked way. I can only share what he has spoken to me through his words and discerned for me through his Holy Spirit. I can only warn others of what I have experienced and have done. The very deceptive ways from within that is masked as knowledge and understanding for self. It is simply how one is self-deceived. I never thought this would be my life. A man that brought two baby girls into the world around the same time with two different women. I never thought I would be the man that dishonored a friend and his wife in their own home during my time of need. I never thought I would be the man that had affairs with married woman. Nor the man that eventually cheated on his own wife while she was pregnant with my son years later. The man that portrayed knowing God during those seasons. Never thinking those ways of living were the direct proof of my lack of knowing God. **I am not ashamed to say that of myself I can do <u>nothing</u> without God**. I have lived a life that does not deserve his very love, grace, or mercy. So, when you read words written by me, may you understand that the spirit of the living God is guiding me. Without reading how God uses the least in this world in **1 Corinthians 1:28-31** and learning about men like David and Paul, I would not comprehend this life considering my past. It has been granted to me to understand the depths of deception I was once in. It is confirmed by the writings of the men in the Holy Bible and the teachings of Jesus Christ. I need not the approval of anyone else that this is needed for those that claim Christ and the lost. I have a requirement upon my life like every follower of Christ, and that is to do everything in the ability he gives me, with his Holy Spirit to honor him with my existence while here on earth. That is knowing God, which is submitting your life to him. The days of glorifying the flesh and its weaknesses are over. The days of seeking others in their weaknesses to comfort me are over. I don't need another brother or sister to struggle to feel comforted in my struggles. I want my spiritual family to be whole and well because that is love. For he saved me from death, so anything associated with death such as sin no longer has permission to reside in me. This is the message I've been sent to give. With the Holy Spirit we can walk in Christ with integrity and honor for that glorifies the Father and proves the new life in him as true. Let no man tell you otherwise because of the weakness of his flesh.

Keep your eyes on Jesus Christ

Be not confused my children and any that may read this. You will not have difficulty finding the baggage that I once had. As for this life, none of this is from my works, nor my knowledge. It is but The Holy Spirit that compels me to understand. It is that same spirit that lives in me. I am but a man. A man that has sinned and made more mistakes and errors in life than I can write here. I ask you not to look to my past as your example, but the purpose of this is for you to look to Christ. If Christ said he of himself can do nothing but it is The Father that speaks and does the things we saw him do, then understand anyone claiming to have power or ability to do wonders or miracles is not from

God. It is God only that wills anything from him to be done in this flesh. The flesh has no power to do his work without his Spirit. **As I close this chapter and book I say be on guard against the casual ways of this world.** It will appear true and good yet examine through scripture if of God. Therefore, acknowledge your sins, and your flaws. If the root of your evil is not dug up and destroyed, then it will continue to live in you having itself still the foundation. Expose them and keep yourself away from them. My children the truth will never cease. Take the day given to you and be thankful for what your Heavenly Father has provided. Focus on the day at hand and be pure mentally. You must desire a pure heart from God. That's what he judges. Your motives, and your intent are truly what's inside of you. Clean your mind with all pure things, so that your thoughts do not give way to wickedness. For surely the Lord has shown mercy to allow any day we live, let alone with ways not of his. So, let us live it with the fear of the Lord and honor him with what he has given.

Be faithful to God for he is faithful. Understand your purpose is to live free from sin and a corrupt conscience. To suffer for God is to recognize the unholy desires your flesh has and to deny them daily. To walk in the light of Christ is to live with honor and respect of the love shown to you by a merciful God. Your life is not your own. We are to die daily to its own wants and ways it has learned from a corrupt world. Speak like a child of the light. Your very words have the power to mold your life into the light or into the darkness in your heart. A man must believe in his heart that God is, and that Christ was sent by him and is his son. If you truly believe this, then it is not a challenging understanding when you read about him being raised from the dead nor his miracles. The Holy Spirit will help you understand his teachings as being perfect along with his life lived. So be firm in your belief as your ways of living display this belief or disbelief. Our Lord made it clear in **John 8:31-32**. Let us remember his words in this scripture. More specifically let us remember the importance of abiding in his word. For this is neglected so often, yet the desire to be made free is always sought after. You cannot have freedom in the truth, nor know it, unless you abide by his word. May all that read this be in the peace from God our Father that sent the Christ our Lord Jesus. In him he defeated death and granted The Holy Spirit to us that believe in him. There is no greater gift, there will be no greater grace or mercy upon anyone's life. There is no greater purpose in our lives. There is no other truth. There is no other Birthright to be received.

If you only remember one thing concerning this book, remember that to follow Christ is to live just as he did. The fact that none of us have means our unworthy lives have experienced his goodness in abundance. This abundance is not what the world sees of value such as money or high-priced materials, although I have witnessed him add to me such things. Rather it is of the Holy Spirit filled truth that is only by his grace and mercy. Remember these words from Christ. Wherever your treasure is there your heart will be also. So, I share the abundance of treasure he has given me with this book. Everyone has a Birthright, we either receive it or we desire temporal things instead of it. How great is the sorrow for the one that believed the lie, the lie that the temporal things were greater than their birthright. How great is the joy for the one who values their birthright and lives their life in honor of it. So, choose today whom you will serve and consider that at the end of every life, we all

served someone.

Shalom

JOHN 8 31-32

<u>If you abide in My word</u>, you
are My disciples indeed. And
you shall know the truth, and
the truth shall make you
free."

Life of Living Christ
LLC

Lifeoflivingchrist.com

@LLChristYeshua

Made in United States
Troutdale, OR
07/04/2024